# CONCEPTUAL IDEALISM

# Conceptual Idealism

NICHOLAS RESCHER

OXFORD
BASIL BLACKWELL
1973

ISBN: 0 631 14950 3
Library of Congress Catalog Card No: 72–96837

Printed in Great Britain by
Western Printing Services Ltd.
Bristol

# ERRATA

(1) Page 127, lines 4-2 from end. This sentence should read as follows: 'Hence, the *diversity* of the now-contents allows us to regard as a fact the < 'transient' division of psychological time into past and future by the > 'now' of conceptualizing awareness.' (The material enclosed in < > was omitted.)

(2) Page 128, Ferré quotation, last sentence. This should read as follows: 'Thus a systematically incoherent division is created between the order of *mental events conceived as occurring tenselessly*, on the one hand, in a perfect democracy of earlier-later relations wherein none has special < claims or privileges, and the order of mental events experienced as > occurring transiently, on the other hand, in a remorselessly ruled public succession of present moments.' (The material enclosed in < > was omitted, and the italicized material was partly set in Roman type.)

(3) Page 129, line 14. Change 'experimental' to 'experiential.'

# CONTENTS

# PREFACE

This book endeavors to formulate and defend a form of idealism of the 'Hegelian' type in the tradition of Green, Bradley, Bosanquet, Royce, McTaggart, and Blanshard. Of course, it departs markedly from the positions of all these writers – it is axiomatic that the agreement of any two philosophers goes only a very brief distance. Apart from any divergences of doctrine, the *conceptual* idealism put forward here differs fundamentally from that of its predecessors in methodology. By basing the argumentation on an appeal to concepts, conceptual schemes, and their linguistic manifestations, it is more keenly attuned to the philosophical ethos of the present than any older version of idealism articulated in the style of an earlier age. I hope (for certainly it is a mere hope rather than an actual expectation) that this development of the idealist case will militate against the facile dismissal of idealism that has become virtually standard in Anglo-American Philosophy since the early part of this century, leading one influential writer to speak disparagingly of 'the temporary and untypical influence of Idealism on British thought.'[1]

[1] Bernard Williams in a review of A. J. Ayer's *Russell and Moore: The Analytical Heritage*, in *The Observer*, 16 May 1971, p. 32. Again, Richard J. Bernstein speaks of British Idealism as 'a brief and unfortunate chapter – a temporary aberration – in the ancient tradition of British empiricism' (*Praxis and Action* [Philadelphia, 1971], pp. 231–2). Both these commentators echo the tones of William James' all too prophetic 1908 Oxford lecture: 'Fortunately, our age seems to be growing philosophical again.... Oxford, long the seed-bed, for the English world, of the idealism inspired by Kant and Hegel, has recently become the nursery of a very different way of thinking.... It looks as if the ancient English empiricism, so long put out of fashion here by nobler sounding germanic formulas, might be repluming itself and getting ready for a stronger flight than ever' (*A Pluralistic Universe* [New York, 1909], p. 3). As though the native isles of George Berkeley needed to be introduced to idealism as the alien invention of latter-day Germans!

The leading influences behind the line of thought of this book are Kant, the later Hegelians, and Peirce. From Kant derives the emphasis upon the *a priori* element present in the conceptual schemes we use in any interpretative depiction of reality. This *a priori* element is, however, viewed as itself built upon a contingent foundation, and legitimated in terms not of necessitarian but of pragmatic considerations. We thus administer our dose of Kant with a heavy admixture of Peirce. Moreover our idealistic contention that the mind's *a priori* contribution to its view of reality manifests itself in the use of concepts that involve some implicit reference to the mental indicates that the relation of our thought to 'mind independent reality' cannot conform to the structure of a correspondence theory, so that a coherentist approach to the criterion of 'truth about reality' is called for. The ideas operative here represent our debt to the Anglo-American neo-Hegelians.

As these remarks might imply, the book has something of an old-fashioned aura about it – in theme if not in method. This is not altogether inappropriate and perhaps not even avoidable in the setting of a deliberate attempt to revitalize a neglected section of philosophical tradition. At any rate, parts of the discussion proceed along paths reminiscent of an older age, before the obsessive urge for simplicity and tidiness during the inter-war period swept a concern with philosophical fundamentals into the background from which it was only gradually to emerge after the Second World War.

The book presents in improved and expanded form a series of lectures on Idealism delivered during the Trinity Term of 1971 in the school of Literae Humaniores of the University of Oxford at the kind invitation of the Sub-Faculty of Philosophy. A good part of its content represents work done during my tenure of a Guggenheim Fellowship in 1970–71. I very much appreciate the cooperation of these institutions. And I am also most grateful to Corpus Christi College for affording me an academic foothold during my stay in Oxford.

While the book predominantly presents new material, Chapters III–IV develop more fully the argument of sections 1–3 of Pt. III of my *Scientific Explanation* (New York, 1970), and there is some inevitable redundancy with this discussion.

Contrary to my wonted practice, I have not appended to this book a bibliography of the literature of its topic, because this has been rendered superfluous by that provided in A. C. Ewing's excellent anthology *The Idealist Tradition* (Glencoe, The Free Press, 1957). One subsequent publication must, however, be mentioned because of its treatment of ideas that lie in the background of various discussions of the present work. I advert to my book on *The Coherence Theory of Truth* (Oxford, The Clarendon Press, 1973). In that work I am at some pains to argue that acceptance of a coherence criterion of (factual) truth does not require espousal of idealism. However, the line of thought of the present book concurs with the great body of idealist tradition that the converse does *not* obtain, and that idealism – at any rate an idealism of the type I am endeavoring to defend – calls for a coherentist approach to the theory of truth.

I want to thank my Pittsburgh colleagues Richard M. Gale and Wilfrid Sellars for their helpful comments on parts of this material. I am also grateful to Miss Kathleen Walsh for patiently preparing the typescript of the book through several revisions, and for helping to see it through the press.

# Chapter I

# CONCEPTUALISTIC IDEALISM

## I. STAGESETTING

Idealism has been effectively dead in Anglo-American philosophy for more than a generation. Among living philosophers of note only a small handful, among whom Brand Blanshard (b. 1892) and A. C. Ewing (b. 1899) are outstanding, have taken a sympathetic and substantially developed stance towards idealism of the traditional British type as inaugurated in England in the heyday of T. H. Green. However, this eclipse of an important sector of philosophical tradition seems to be entirely unjustified on the merits. The present discussion will endeavor to set up a scaffolding of considerations sympathetic to idealism, attempting to state and defend certain idealist positions in a contemporarily more accessible idiom.

Idealism takes many forms. There is the *spiritualism* of some Eastern philosophers to the effect that everything in the world is made of a spiritual stuff. There is the *ontological* idealism of Berkeley, denying the existence of matter, and maintaining that the only existing things are minds and their conceptions. There is the *transcendental* idealism of Kant, who maintains that the reality of material things is as objects of thought (the 'empirical reality' of physical objects) and insists we must remain agnostic regarding any existence outside the conditions imposed by the mechanisms of our knowledge. Moreover, there is the *absolute* idealism of Bradley and other Hegelians, maintaining that whatever exists is somehow the product of thought – not yours or mine, to be sure, but that of an all-embracing world-mind in which our finite minds are somehow subsumed.

Our own position differs decidedly from all of these, but approaches closest to that of Kant, who, for this reason, frequently provides a point of reference for comparison and contrast. Certainly we do not propose to defend spiritualism, nor absolute idealism for that matter. Nor is there any intention here to argue the ontological thesis that only minds are real and all else is mere appearance. Rather, the discussion seeks to motivate the fundamentally *conceptual* point that mind-involving conceptions play an essential role in the framework of concepts we standardly employ in presenting our view of the world.

In very rough outline the general structure of the position to be argued looks as follows:

(1) Whenever and however we conceive of the particulars that constitute some sector of natural reality, we do so by means of the specific conceptualizing mechanisms that we ourselves *bring* to the cognitive situation.

(2) This conceptional machinery – through its own nature – conditions, canalizes, and in some ways restricts *how* we represent things to ourselves in thought and discourse. This has the consequence that, through its deployment of specific conceptual mechanisms, the mind *in part determines* (i.e. significantly shapes and influences) the materials of knowledge. Put into information-processing terms – with the usual picture of inputs, transformational mechanisms, and outputs – this leads to the upshot that in all our attempts to portray reality the output is a function not of the 'external' inputs alone, but of the mind's transformational mechanisms as well. Thus far, we have moved only towards the position of *rationalism*, the view that the knower makes an active and substantively nontrivial contribution to the constitution of knowledge. But we move beyond rationalism to idealism proper in maintaining that:

(3) In the standard case, the conceptual machinery we make use of is mind-involving, in that it applies conceptions whose adequate specification involves reference to mental operations and processes. That is, the full explanatory articulation of these conceptions requires some mention of operations which – like seeing, or discriminating, or making hypotheses – are specifically characteristic of minds (in the quite obvious sense that anything of which we say that it sees or discriminates or makes hypotheses will be something of which we must be prepared to say that it is or has a mind).

Thus, the general position to be argued here might properly be characterized as *conceptual idealism*. It maintains that the concepts we standardly employ in constituting our view of reality – even extramental, material reality – involve an essential (though generally tacit) reference to minds and their capabilities. This view is not a causal doctrine: it does *not* hold that 'knowledge [of nature] is possible only because of the affinity between the mind of man and the mind which stands behind, and indeed makes, nature.'[1] Rather, ours is a *conceptual* idealism in holding that nature, as we standardly conceive it, is conceived by us in terms of reference whose adequate analysis or explication requires some reference to the characteristically mental processes like imagining, supposing, and the like. On this view, what the mind 'makes' is not nature itself, but the mode-and-manner-determining categories in terms of which we conceive it. Accordingly, it is maintained that the mind shapes (rather than 'makes' pure and simple) not nature *itself*, but nature as it is *for us*. Historically, all forms of idealism have insisted upon the role of mind in the constitution of the world. In this generic sense, our present version of idealism conforms to the pattern of the tradition – although it specifically regards this constitutive role of mind in neither ontological nor causal terms, but in conceptual ones.

## 2. THE ROLE OF A CONCEPTUAL FRAMEWORK

One must inevitably use *the descriptive mechanisms of a conceptual framework* to sort the products of our experience into conceptual pigeon-holes that represent at a very basic level a view – deeply ingrained in our cultural tradition – of how things work in the world. Accordingly, we standardly employ the concept of causality rather than that of animism or that of occult influence; group all occurrences into a neat temporal pattern of past/present/future; cross-classify the people with whom we interact into types on such lines as tribe, family, age, occupation; etc. Some examples of such frameworks of conceptual scaffolding

[1] See W. H. Walsh, describing the position of T. H. Green, in *Hegelian Ethics* (New York, 1969), p. 70.

B

used by the mind in structuring its 'contacts' with the world into actual experiences are provided by the following:

- patterns of order or matrices for relatedness (space, time, causality, taxonomies [similarity-in-point-of], the Gestalt organization of perception)
- the taxonomic organization of experience (colors, the taxonomy of animals, the classification of elements, the functional groupings of artifacts, etc.)
- explanatory frameworks and the conception of scientific explanation
- the complex of social categories and roles
- intentionality and purpose (behavior vs. action; the concept of a person [man/animal/machine])
- evaluative categories: value (importance, interest), norms and standards

Descriptive and classificatory ordering mechanisms of this sort constitute the conceptual frameworks with which we come duly armed by our cultural tradition to the task of rationally structuring our experience. We humans can dispense in our thought about things with such descriptive and categorical frameworks to no greater extent than we can convey information without language or calculate without symbolic devices.

Reality – 'our reality,' as we can and do view it – is a 'mental construct' built up in the transaction of experiential encounter of person and environment by means of a conceptual framework that invariably and inevitably makes essential use of organizing principles. Such principles are *a priori*, if only in the relative sense that we must already have them in hand in any situation of cognitively meaningful experience. But, to be sure, they are not 'innate' in the human intellect. Nor can they simply be read off from the world about us by some concept-free observational process of 'mere inspection.' (Indeed with observation and inspection it is already 'too late' to reach them, since – as Kant insisted – 'raw experience' uncooked by conceptualization is not possible.)

Now the pivotal concepts of explanation and description that are standardly deployed in forming our conception of reality –

concepts like time, causality, and possibility – all have ramifications that are, as will be argued, at bottom mind-dependent. To speak figuratively, the picture of reality that we make for ourselves is painted in mind-involving colors. What is mind-dependent here is not *reality itself* (whatever *that* might be), but reality-as-we-picture-it: not reality *an sich*, but *our* reality. When one looks at something through colored lenses this works so as to condition '*what* we see' (in one sense of this expression) by its determination, or rather partial determination, of *how* we see it. It will be argued that a precisely analogous point holds when one treats of objects in speech and thought by the deployment of conceptual mechanisms, and specifically those of mind-invoking sort.

Insofar as mind can effect its intellectual grasp upon 'objective, mind-independent reality,' it can do so only through the mediate deployment of its conceptual mechanisms of representation. However, the conceptual machinery we standardly use (and the descriptive language within which it is embedded) is an intellectual construction that at virtually all key points betrays its mind-originated character: it is laden throughout with references – overt or covert – to the capabilities and workings of minds. Accordingly, the (language-embedded) conceptual framework we standardly deploy in thought and discourse about reality is a mind-created artifact whose component elements are in certain ways fundamentally mind-involving, and in whose applications this invocation of mind is everpresent and not to be shaken off. (Here, as elsewhere in this introductory chapter, a brief, preliminary exposition may seem telegraphic to the point of obscurity, and is at best no more than a sign-post towards the fuller treatment of the subsequent discussion.)

We do not and cannot 'apprehend reality' directly, without use of the descriptive mechanisms afforded by language and the conceptual scheme that goes with it. As W. V. Quine cogently insists, there is no 'cosmic exile' who can view the world in an altogether detached, objective point-of-view-less way. Art historians – E. H. Gombrich most prominently – have insisted that no painter can look at, conceive, or represent nature directly 'as it really is'; he has to work within some established framework of defined images, symbols, and schemata which he may then modify and adopt to his own purposes. And this is true all the more of our cognitive re-creations of natural things in conscious thought. Any facet of reality must, if conceived at all, be conceived of from a conceptual point of view. And the fundamental scheme of concepts we standardly deploy, with its reference to individual particulars, space, time, and causality, is – as the ensuing discussion will try to exhibit in detail – fundamentally mind-invoking. Our picture of reality is, to put it figuratively, painted with the coloration of mind.

### 3. THE 'STANDARD CONCEPTUAL SCHEME'

One methodological point must be stressed. There will be no attempt here to argue transcendentally that *any* conceptual framework that affords a basis for a conception of reality *must* in the conceptual nature of things be mind-involving. This extremely ambitious thesis may, for aught I know, have some merit. But be this as it may, it is not something whose truth will be maintained here. Rather it will be my (quite sufficiently ambitious) aim to argue that the basic concepts we actually do employ *de facto* (and which the Western intellectual tradition has predominantly and standardly employed, both in science and in everyday life) in framing our usual conception of nature – as a complex of physical particulars located in space and time and interacting causally – are each and every one of them fundamentally mind-involving. Accordingly, it is totally beside the point that, quite trivially, *any* conceptual framework is inevitably mind-related in that it is a *conceptual* scheme, and only minds can operate with concepts. The mind-involvingness at issue does not hinge on the trivial fact that a conceptual scheme is at issue, but on the weightier consideration of the *sort* of conceptual scheme it is, and of the substantive materials that it affords.

The following objection might be launched against this approach:

Let it be granted (for the sake of discussion) that the analysis has established the fundamentally idealist nature of our ordinary conceptual scheme, our standard stance of reality that views nature as a fabric of particulars in space and time interacting causally. But what does this relative appropriateness of idealism as a theory apropriate *for this conceptual scheme* show about the correctness of idealism *as such*? Perhaps the ordinary scheme is somehow inappropriate or even just plain wrong. Indeed, perhaps the very success of the argument in showing its idealistic commitments does no more than to establish the inappropriateness of this conceptual scheme. Very possibly, this whole ordinary view of the world is just misguided.

It is, to be sure, perfectly possible that what we have termed the 'standard conceptual scheme' is untenable and needs to be replaced. To shunt this prospect aside is unsatisfactory and high-handed. Of course, a conceptual scheme can be given up in favor of another. The issue becomes, in the final analysis, one of cost-benefit evaluation: what would be gained and what lost? If the standard scheme did not have some (nonhistorical) claims to preeminence, we would scarcely be justified in granting it the position of prominence and centrality that our method accords to it. We must thus grapple with the problem of how the 'standard' conceptual scheme – with its heavy infusion of mind-invoking elements – can make good its claims upon us. The issue of the legitimation of this scheme in the context of our present philosophical purposes is crucial for the justification of our methodology.

The answer, in a nutshell, is this: since philosophical problems and disputes arise in and relate to the standard conceptual framework, this framework constitutes the foundation of relevancy with which all clarifications of philosophical issues must at some point be connected. We are concerned with *philosophical* issues, and the entire problem-context of the philosophical discussion of 'the things of this world' relates to and arises within the concept-framework of the ordinary perspective. So if some *other* perspective is pressed upon us we may pose the dilemma:

(1) EITHER the new conceptual perspective agrees with the old (i.e., the 'standard') one, so that in *this* case the old

problems are still with us and await a solution 'on their own terms.'

(2) OR the new conceptual perspective departs from and in essential respects disagrees with the old. But then we haven't *resolved* the problems that arose in the old context at all, we have simply *abandoned* them, and have gone on to talk about something else.

The focus of discussion is thus 'our' world, the world-as-we-regard-it, conceptualized in accordance with the standard conceptual scheme of thing and attribute, object and space-time position, person and capacity, cause and effect. We have to begin from where we are. If we want to talk about the issues as the philosophical tradition sees them, then we must proceed from the standard conceptual scheme. To go to a different conceptual scheme is literally 'to change the subject' – not to speak of the same thing better but to speak about something else. Nothing, of course, can be said against someone who prefers something else (somebody who would, for example, rather do Egyptology than philosophy). But in the context of philosophical discussion to talk of Egyptology is to commit not an actual error, to be sure, but merely the fallacy of ignoring the question at issue (*ignoratio elenchi*).

These considerations as to the foundational role of the standard conceptual perspective may serve to validate an emphatic concern with what I have termed our 'standard view' of natural reality, as a congeries of physical particulars emplaced in space and time and interacting causally. The ensuing discussion will in large measure be devoted to articulating various consequences of the presuppositions and (largely tacit) theses and claims built into the conceptual scheme at issue in this standard view. We shall try to bring to light certain mind-invoking aspects of all the fundamental concepts involved here: particularly, space, time, causality, and others.

(The methodologically sensitive reader may well inquire: 'Just how is one to conceive of such an inquiry? Are you engaged upon *a priori* conceptual analysis or an empirical investigation of the sociology of Weltanschauungen?' The answer is that our inquiry is composite, and combines both factual [empirical] and analytical [*a priori*] considerations. There can be no question that our 'standard' view of reality is the product of evolutionary development that incorporates and reflects in its presuppositions our human vision of how things work in the world. What this view involves and what its constituent theses and presuppositions are, are empirical matters, and empirical data are certainly relevant to any clarification of its details. This empirical dimension makes the inquiry a fundamentally amphibious admixture of conceptual and factual considerations. But still, the great bulk of the discussion will have to be given to an analysis of conceptual involvements, and this fact means that the over-all discussion will be heavily weighted on the analytical side.)

### 4. THE BASIS OF MIND-INVOLVEMENT

The contributory role of mind in the formation of our view of the-world-as-we-know-it inheres in the fact that a variety of very different conceptual frameworks can with equal validity be superimposed upon the order of 'empirical fact' – even as a given empirical circumstance can be presented under very different descriptions. Descriptive information about the empirical features of things is always in part a product of mental contrivance. Take a simple example, say, 'The cat is on the mat.' Consider such obvious alternatives as: 'Smith's newest pet is on the doormat,' 'The neighborhood nuisance is in its favorite spot.' Even in so crude a case, it is clear the conceiving mind contributes (1) the 'botanizing' of experience inherent in the application of classificatory concepts (cats, mats) (2) the identification of specific particulars (*that* cat, *this* mat), and (3) the application of relational qualifiers ('is physically emplaced upon'). Throughout such cases, the mind brings a certain machinery of conceptualization to bear, machinery not dictated by (or simply 'to be read off from') a concept-neutral inspection of reality (if that were possible!), but constructed on the basis of the mind's experimental interaction with the world in human experience.

Any experiential encounter with physical reality is thus significantly *underdeterminative* of the conceptualized perception that 'results' from it in human cognition. The 'reality' that is encountered does not of itself determine (causally or otherwise) how we are to think of it, independently of the apparatus of thought that we for our part bring to the transaction. There are always many possibilities here – depending on the conceptual framework that is not only an indispensable factor in this transaction – but one that must be *brought to* it by the experiencing agent. Diverse alternatives arise here not only in regard to different means for description and individuation but also – and especially – in regard to different views as to 'how things work in the world.' (For example, the savage who sees a jet plane pass high overhead might perfectly well think of its contrail as an integral *part* of the flying object he sees.)

Some useful examples of how the mind contributes *substantively* to the 'internal content' of a perception can be given with reference to the following:

DOG/dog

كلب

Ke(((ogs

We 'cannot help' seeing the first line as words and letters, and indeed see that the *same* word is merely repeated. We 'cannot bring ourselves' really to see that first pair of inscriptions as merely a collection of abstract shapes. On the other hand, the second line (Arabic for 'dog') is simply an abstract pattern for us: the 'untrained eye' finds it hard to persuade itself that this could possibly be seen in any other light. Finally, in the third line with its banana-letters (taken from a cereal advertisement by a firm we assume to be familiar), it is striking that there is no difficulty in seeing the bananas *as letters* in this context. In all such cases, the mind's eye leaps without hesitation to the appropriately 'symbolic' interpretation. And this is perfectly paradigmatic in perception. (To repeat, all this is simply Kant's thesis of the essential inseparability of perception from conceptualizing thought.)

We do not experience 'things as they are,' but always take note of them from the angle of some conceptual perspective.

We apprehend their duly framework-relativized conceptualized 'meaning'. We do not (may not) see white fluid but rather milk; we hear not a dim hooting but a distant train.

All this, of course, is maximally evident with respect to those items that are themselves of a symbolic character. Consider

$$a, \; A, \; a$$

We unhesitatingly apprehend all these inscriptions as the letter A. But why? Certainly not because of any *physical* similarity – let alone an identity of structure. Rather, what is at issue is their *functional* equivalence through the workings of the symbolic process. Their classificatory unity is an intellectual product. (It certainly has a physical basis, but this basis is not determinative but only delimitative.)

The conceptual mechanism of representation fundamentally conditions our perception of things. Seeing, for example, is always seeing-that: we never experience seeing something without 'seeing something *as* such-and-such' and so 'seeing *that* it is such-and-such.' We not only see upturned lips and furrowed brows but cheerful smiles and worried faces: All perception involves an element of interpretation. We thus come back to the insistence of all idealists since Berkeley that seeing is not *just* an optical-physiologic process, because, while we look at things with the eyes of the body, we see them with the *mind's eye*. (Note the dual aspect of the English word 'regard' as *look at* and as *estimate* or *esteem*.) Whenever we see something, the issue of how we see it always has a conceptual component. (On the empirical background see R. L. Gregory, *The Intelligent Eye* [London, 1970].)

We, of course, always use symbols in describing, but we also often describe things *in symbolic terms*, with clear implications as to what these things 'stand for' and 'mean.' We not only use symbols in describing (conceiving) reality but describe (conceive) reality in symbolic terms (standing for . . . as-if . . . X-like . . . (Y-ish).) Symbolism is one key paradigm: Not only symbols *per se* (A, α, etc.) but everything that we apprehend *means* something against the background of a conceptual scheme, and *meaning* is, of course, the fundamental category of mind. The entire conception of symbolic function (standing for, representation) is inherently mentalistic: there can only be representation *for a mind*. 'Taking one thing as equivalent with another' is as inherently mentalistic as imagining or supposing.

The workings of the symbolic process invade all of our conceptualized apprehension of things.[2] We invariably think of them – 'symbolically' as it were – under a certain description or classification. All conceptualizing calls for assimilation and as such deploys the familiar (though not wholly understood) intellectual machinery of comparison and contrast. This typological affinitizing of things to one another is inherently mentalistic: it involves emphasizing some aspects and neglecting others (abstraction), and it is a point of principle that only minds are capable of emphasis and neglect.

Now whenever the symbolic or associative function enters in, the work of mind is particularly evident. For here – as the example of letters of the alphabet shows – *the conceptualizing experience* we have of it is of constitutive or formative importance for the object conceptualized. And consequently the seemingly natural distinction between what is experienced and our patently mentalistic *experience* – between the *what* and the *how* of our experience – loses its seeming decisiveness, the *how* entering into the determination of the *what*. (If I do not see the isolated configuration *as* a letter, then *what* I see is – at least in the first approximation – not a letter at all, but merely a shape of a certain sort.) In this special case we encounter mind-invocation with exemplary clarity.

The point is that we think even of nonmental things in mind-invoking terms, so that even when 'what we think of' is mind-remote, '*the item as*' it presents is not. It is not just that our *minds* think of things, for that's trivial, but that we standardly do think of them in mind-invoking terms of reference.

[2] Note should be taken that it is not being said that the dogs and other intelligent animals apprehend things in a symbolically conceptualized manner. We are not arguing a *transcendental* thesis as to how anything whatever must do its apprehending, but a *de facto* thesis how we humans actually go about it. For us it takes a conceptual scheme to identify particular objects, and we think of the natural particulars we encounter in our experience in the symbolic/conceptual mode, regardless of how dogs, for example, may 'think' of them.

The critical consideration is not just the generic and transcendental fact that *some* conceptual scheme is inevitably needed as vehicle for thought about 'the real world,' but the specific fact that the conceptual scheme which we *de facto* standardly use in thinking of it as we do (as a collection of physical particulars, characterizable by a descriptive framework of empirical properties, located in space and time, and interacting causally) is laden throughout with mind-involving conceptions.

Let us sketch the line of argument. It will be maintained that what we have characterized as the standard conceptual scheme deploys as its fundamental ideas concepts whose analysis will ultimately bring to light an implicit reference to minds. Accordingly, it is a critical fact about this scheme that such mentalistic involvements characterize its range of concepts: Its main conceptions are 'theoretical constructs' among whose constituents mentalistic components can be discerned. But this *extra-theoretical* fact need not reflect *intra-theoretically*. Once we have entered within the concept-domain of the theory no further element of internally *overt* reference to minds need be present. Accordingly, this involvement of mind need not be explicit and so *internal* to the set of concepts involved, but may represent an *external* fact about this conceptual apparatus (in the sense of Rudolf Carnap's well-known distinction between internal and external questions). When specifying a property (e.g., the color) of, say, an apple, one is not saying anything overtly about minds, but they may enter in covertly: reddish (= red-seeming) is a perfectly good color description, even though the color-indication involved is presented in obliquely mind-referring terms. Our conceptual approach sees the invocation of mind at the level of what is implicit in the *machinery of discourse* within the standard conceptual framework, not at the level of what is explicitly said when this machinery is used.

## 5. AN IMMEDIATE OBJECTION

Faced with an idealistic position (of *any* sort) it might seem tempting to argue as follows:

Idealism rests on a *fallacy of insufficient distinction*. To take an idealist position is to obliterate the significant difference between

(1) an *X* (i.e., a stick or stone or bit of sealing wax)

on the one hand, and on the other

(2) the thought (perception, imagination, etc.) of an *X*.

This latter item is, of course, quite obviously and in general mind-dependent. Now what the idealist does is just to confuse this latter mind-dependency with the situation in the former case; he fails to draw a sufficient distinction between *things* and the *thoughts* of things.

So goes the charge.

Now it is quite conceivable that some idealists have committed the error here at issue (and a very real error it is). But to establish this would certainly not be enough for the opponent's purposes. For the charge has it that idealism *in general* rests on this fallacy, and that is a difficult case to make out. After all, what the intelligent idealist wants to maintain is certainly not just that *thoughts-about-X*'s are mind-dependent, for this is trivial and goes without saying, but that in certain crucial cases the very things as they are at issue in these thoughts — and not just the *thoughts* of them — are mind-referring. Traditionally, mirages and after-images and colors (i.e., phenomenal colors) have been the idealist's paradigms. It is not just that *thoughts* of mirages and after-images and colors are mind-dependent, but that the mirages and after-images and colors *themselves* are. Thus (for example) we cannot even specify or identify an odor without saying how something 'smells' — and so without bringing a mind-involving capability into the picture. (Even when we merely say that something 'has the smell of a dried-out orange' there is a crucial albeit tacit *addendum*: 'to an olefactorily normal person under ordinary circumstances.')

One obviously can and must distinguish between things and the thoughts-of-things. Some idealists have perhaps, on occasion, confused the two, but the type of idealism to be espoused here is *not* one that commits this confusion. The standard tactics here will *not* be to argue for the mind-relatedness of certain things as such and *per se*, but rather to maintain the mind-relatedness of these items under their standard identifying characterizations, arguing this on the ground that these characterizations are mind-involving.

Our argument thus does not commit the facile fallacy of reasoning (say) that since physical objects can only be *known* by mind, they can exist only for mind. Rather we argue that the *way* in which they are known by mind – the conceptual framework of reference in terms of which one standardly conceptualizes them – is such that as conceived *in these mind-invoking terms* they can exist only for mind.

## 6. THE NATURE OF CONCEPTUAL MIND-INVOLVEMENT

Thus, according to the position espoused here, it is not 'the thing itself' – whatever *that* might be – that is mind-involvement, but 'the thing *as we think of it*,' that is 'the thing under a certain characterization.' For a careful distinction must be drawn in the present connection between

(1) the mind-involvement of a specified *item X*

and

(2) the mind-involvement of a *specification* of the *item x.*

If Henry Higginbottom is the most generally disliked member of the group then it is clear that the specification or identification represented by the definite description

'the most generally disliked member of the group'

is mind-involving. Dislike being an essentially mind-correlative circumstance, it follows directly that the indicated code of identification is also essentially mind-involving. But this, of course, would not of itself mean that the *man* Henry Higginbottom is somehow mind-dependent. The fact that an item *can* be identified by a mind-involving description would not render it mind-involving in any interesting sense, since presumably *anything* can be so indicated – for instance by referring to it as 'the thing we were just talking about.' The mind-involvement of a thing could only be established in some meaningful way if – as we shall maintain within a scope of considerable generality – the *standard* way of identifying it were somehow mind-involving. (And, of course, it is so *a fortiori* when *every* adequate identification of it is mind-involving, as is plainly the case with such extreme examples as headaches, mirages, and the like.) The presently crucial point is that an identification may be so articulated in terms (perhaps tacitly) of concepts that mind-involvement inheres in *machinery of formulation* (i.e., arises from the implicit use of mentalistic concepts) rather than deriving from *the facts formulated*.[3] A concept is mind-involving in the present, conceptualistic sense if its full and adequate explication – not just on the side of its semantical meaning-content, but also on that of its applicability-conditions – cannot be carried out without some reference to those functions which, like thinking, imagining, assuming, etc., are characteristic capabilities of minds.[4]

Our position is concerned only obliquely with the *ontological* question of whether or not certain items can exist as apart from cognition[5] and with the *epistemological* question of what we can know about such items. In saying that something is 'mind-involving' one must distinguish between

(1) *the item that* is cognized
(2) *the item as* it is cognized

We refrain from any directly ontological consideration of the 'mind-dependency' of (1) in any manner that severs it altogether from (2), because it is recognized that the only conceptual path

[3] Any strictly conventional system of location, for example, one based on idealized reference points such as geographical coordinates (or even North/South/East/West), is obviously mind-dependent. This fact suffices to invalidate Bertrand Russell's confident claim that 'Edinburgh is north of London' is a paradigm instance of a relational fact that has no trace of mind-dependency about it. (See *The Problems of Philosophy* [Oxford, 1912], p. 153.)

[4] Accordingly, our deliberations call for only relatively modest data from the theory of mind. No specific features of the mind as an entity of a certain sort are required. All that we need a schedule of 'paradigmatically mental activities' like conceiving, hypothesizing, etc., together with the thesis that anything that engages in these is or has a mind.

[5] The thrust of Berkeley's dictum "'tis wondrous to contemplate the world emptied of intelligences' (*Commonplace Book*, no. 23) *as he understood it* is simply not an issue for our species of idealism.

towards the very specification of (1) goes by way of (2). Our concern throughout is with (2), and seeks to show that the very mode and manner of the conception of natural particulars within our standard conceptual scheme is mind-invoking. And since any (1)-item must lie outside cognitive reach save insofar as it corresponds to a (2)-item, the (soon to be argued for) standard mind-involvement of this latter will be quite sufficient for our purpose of showing the mind-involvement of things *as we know them.*

The entry of mind into the framework of our considerations must be clarified. As has been stressed repeatedly, it is neither ontological (which would be too far-fetched), nor epistemological (which would be too trivial), but conceptual. Our method endeavors to use the analytical unraveling of concepts in bringing to light an implicit reference to characteristically mental processes. Some crude examples are: pleasing, painful, reddish. *Pleasing* involves reference to a 'state of mind' (being pleased), a *headache* represents a condition of mind (it requires feeling pain of a certain sort), to be *reddish* a thing must be red-*seeming* and so make a certain impact upon minds. Again, in speaking of a '*fearful* storm' we say something about the storm (viz., that it is fear-inspiring) that makes this conception essentially mind-referring. But more subtle cases also arise, for example phenomenal color and metrical length. In characterizing something as red we may well maintain no more than what is needed for showing that it *would* appear red to normal observers in standard circumstances. In asserting a distance to be 5 miles we are saying that a particular result would ensue *if* a certain measuring operation were to be carried out – and this (viz., measuring) is a mind-involving operation since it involves noting, remembering, counting, etc. In cases of this sort our concepts are such as to indicate in implicitly mind-referring terms of reference the states of affairs that must obtain (actually or hypothetically) if an adequate warrant is to exist for the claims made by their means.

Thus in explicating the types of conceptual mind-involvement, it is useful to draw the distinction between

(i) the *ontological mind-dependency* that arises when – as with headache or worries – the analytically revealed reference to mind is such as to warrant the contention that the very existence of the items at issue hinges on the existence of minds (whence the nomenclature of 'ontological').

(ii) the (merely) *conceptual mind-invokingness* that arises when a reference to mind in present in the conceptual perspective from which the item at issue is viewed; when mentalistic references are implicit in the conceptual machinery of consideration rather than explicit in the very nature of the object being considered.

In the typical and characteristic cases, we encounter *ontological* mind-dependency when dealing with aspects or features of minds themselves (e.g., a headache), or when dealing with what is somehow a product of the workings of minds, even if not in itself mind-pertaining (e.g., a worry). By contrast, a merely *conceptual* mind-invocation obtains when the involvement of mind, though real, is less immediate and direct. In the former case the reference to mind is relatively immediate and overt in the very meaning of the concept; in the latter case it is a relatively oblique and covert facet of its usability.

Throughout, it is important to note that what is at issue is *not* the trivializing fact that a certain concept is applied – trivial because concept-application is always and inevitably a function of mind – but the mind-involving nature of the circumstances that must obtain when this specific concept is appropriately to be applicable in a certain instance. We have in view here concepts such as those whose use calls for processes, like inspection or measurement, that, upon due analysis, can be seen to be implicitly but inherently mind-referring. The crucial issue is not the (trivially mind-involving) one of *that* a concept can only be used by mind-endowed beings, but rather of *how* it is used by them – i.e., with or without essentially relying upon mind-involving paradigms or operations.

The nature of the mind-invocation at issue in our theory needs further classification. Several points are crucial here:

(1) *The mind-involvement at issue is conceptual:* it has to do with the concepts we standardly employ in the individuation

and description of natural objects (either as to their content or their conditions of applicability). The pivotal point of the idealism that concerns us is not the trivial one that minds are needed for something to be conceptualized, but the more subtle idea that a reference to minds may be built implicitly into the very mode and manner in which this conceptualization is framed. When we conceive of something, there is – over and above the obvious fact *that* we conceptualize it mentalistically – room for the wholly additional question of *how* it is conceptualized; and here, at this inner level of contentual reference, there may also be an indication of minds. Consider, for example, such descriptive characterizations 'red-appearing,' 'red-seeming,' 'red-looking' or 'reddish,' all of which indicates how a visible object *would strike* an observer.

The possession of mind-involving features is no monopoly of the unreal. Perfectly real sunsets can be *reddish* (i.e., red-appearing), perfectly real clouds can be *roundish* (i.e., round-seeming), a perfectly real dog can be of *wolf-like* appearance (i.e., readily mistakable for a wolf). While indicating actual features of seen objects every bit as much as their outright characterization as simply *red*, they nevertheless couch these features in essentially mind-referring terms. (They thus differ, at least on the surfaces of it, from such characterizations as *green* or *round*.) Characteristics such as being 'roundish' or 'wolf-like' or 'intricate' are not absolute properties of objects. These characterizations are fundamentally *relational*, having to do not just with the 'objective' properties but also with the reactions of observers, i.e., with the sort of impression a mind obtains with respect to that object. Characterizations of this sort have a conceptual content that would make no sense if one abstracted wholly from the capacities and capabilities of minds. The mind-involvement at issue here is a matter not of the 'external facts' but of the internal *terms of reference* of what is being said.

Perhaps the most favorable paradigm example of mind-involvement is – as already suggested – an inscription of 'a letter of the alphabet.' If an imprint of the proper structure and shape came about by the chance play of natural processes this would not qualify it as a letter of the alphabet. One cannot give an

C

adequate explanation of what is at issue in a letter of the alphabet without a relativization to language – i.e., to symbol systems employed by comprehending minds: in a languageless setting there cannot be letters of the alphabet. The very concept in view is such that any adequate account of the matter must in the ultimate analysis make reference to minds and their capabilities and activities – no matter how covert or tacit such reference may be 'in the first analysis.' In an utterly mind-abstractive setting of discussion – one denuded of all mentalistic character-izations – the concept of a letter of the alphabet or an odor or an ache could have no place, for the very concept at issue requires looking at something from a mind-invoking perspective. The need for an at least hypothetical recourse to minds in their analysis shows that such concepts are mind-involving.

The point at issue here can be clarified by an adaptation of Carnap's well-known distinction between what he calls internal and external questions.[6] Assume it to be conceded that the present thesis is correct, and that an analysis of certain pivotal conceptions of our conceptual scheme – carried out from a perspective external to this scheme itself, so that entry *within* the scheme has not yet been effected, with its conditions and presuppositions regarding conceptual relationships yet up for explicit review, because still ungranted – may show them to be in certain respects mind-involving. But once one pays the entry-fee of this externally re-vealed mind-involvingness, no *further* internal reference to minds is necessary. For example if (as we shall argue) causation is con-ceptually mind-invoking, this fact does not prevent 'fire produces smoke' from being about fire and smoke and the relations be-tween them in a 'perfectly objective' way. The mind-invocation that can be seen – from the perspective of an external vantage-point – to be built into the machinery of our conceptual scheme does not mentalize the truths we formulate by its means. To enter into the conceptual scheme is to adopt certain mind-referential devices. But once this entry is effected and the conceptual per-

---

[6] See Rudolf Carnap, *Meaning and Necessity* (Chicago, 1947; 2nd ed., 1956), supplement A, sect. 2 (of the 2nd ed.). Note, however, that whereas Carnap envisages this distinction as drawn with respect to *languages*, we here draw it with respect to the *conceptual schemes* that they embody.

spective of the scheme assured, then there is not, in general, any further and, so to speak, *overt* reference to mind in our claims about the world. So the externalized aspects of mind-invocation of the scheme do not spill over into any internal claims of a functional role for mind in the ordinary course of things.

The mind-invokingness of the elements of a conceptual scheme are thus *external* facts about it. Thus it can only be said from an external perspective that I am 'formulating a claim in terms of a mentalistic frame of reference.' From the internal *standpoint*, I am simply 'stating how something in fact is – really and objectively is.' The invocation of mind is the entry fee, as it were, that we pay for ingress into the sphere of the conceptual scheme; once *there*, no additional mind-dependency need attach to the theses we frame by use of these concepts. This difference between the internal, mechanism-ignoring and external, mechanism-conscious standpoint is crucial for our purposes throughout the book. For when we say that the use of some concept involves a mind-invoking commitment, we do not mean that this commitment need form part of the actual *intention* of the user of the concept; we simply say that a depth analysis of its usage shows that such a commitment is there as part of the total situation, even though any recognition of it may be lacking.

(2) *Mind-involvement not causal or historical.* This conceptual recourse to mind is not a matter of natural history. The issue is not one of there being minds in the world or not. We are not concerned with issues regarding the evolutionary history of the world: it is *not* being held that the mind-dependent aspects of nature 'sprung into being' with the evolution of mind – any more than colors sprung into being with the evolution of eyes. Something 'reddish' does not become so with the entry of minds on the stage of universal history. The question in hand is not one of causality at all: minds themselves do not somehow cause the seen object to become roundish (but not round) or line-like (but not linear). The shape or color at issue is not 'created' by minds. The issue is not one of *causality*, but one of *meaning*, and more specifically of the conceptual characterization in view. Consider an analogy. The causal fact that we require a blade for making a knife is beside the point; for the crux lies in the *conceptual* fact

that unless that thing attached to the handle were not (properly to be characterized as) a blade, then the complex just would not be (properly characterized as) a knife. It is this sort of conceptual involvement that is operative in our discussion. To signalize this *conceptual* involvement of mind we generally use the label 'mind-invoking' for the type of mind-involvement at issue, to distinguish it from the outright 'mind-dependency' of those stronger, *onto-logical* (rather than *conceptual*) ramifications of mind of which hopes and worries are paradigmatic.

(3) *Mind-involvement not psychological or voluntaristic or in any way idiosyncratic.* The mind-involvement at issue here is not something psychological in any subjective sense regarding a person's characteristic tendency to 'see' things in a certain way. Unlike being 'pleasing' or 'frightening' or 'familiar' the feature of an object as being 'reddish' or 'box-like' is not in the first instance a question of a person's subjective history but of the 'objective' features of things.

In speaking of mind-involvement or mind-invocation, no reference to any particular mind is at issue. The mental aspect here operative is not private or personal: it is not a question of *whose* mind — of this or that mind rather than another. The dependence at issue is wholly generic and systematic in nature. Thus phenomenal colors are mind-involving in that they have to do with the *looks* of things, and only minds can be looked-to in a literal sense; the language of looking is only figuratively applicable to mirrors or receiving instruments.

Again, the mind-relatedness in view is not something volun-taristic, something over which persons have power and which can be changed around by their thinking ('wishful' or otherwise). To say something (e.g., a color) is mind-involving is not to say that it is illusory or delusory or otherwise 'unreal'; it is not to say that it is psychological in any subjective, person-relative sense; it is not to say that it is arbitrary, choice-related, or changeable by human discretion. The idealist theory of nature is not a do-it-yourself view that lets us shape the world in any way we please. Historically, idealists have never made a reality a matter of wish-ful thinking that lets thought shape the world without objective constraints. Constraints have always been recognized: God (in

Berkeley), the faculty-structure of the mind (in Kant), biological and perhaps ultimately Darwinian considerations (in Spencer), have played the restrictive role that an objectively given conceptual scheme plays on our own view. Thus the items we characterize as 'mind-dependent' can be perfectly interpersonal and objective; they need not be subjective at all − let alone be something over which people have voluntaristic control.

The pivotal point is that certain key properties ascribed to things in the standard conceptual scheme are at bottom *relational* properties with some facet of 'the mind' (or of minds-in-general) as one term of this relation. And there is nothing whatsoever *unreal* about such mentalesque properties (*dog-like* is just as 'real' a characterization as *feline*). But these properties − though perfectly *real* and perfectly independent of anyone's idiosyncratic wishes, desires, impressions, etc., − are yet mind-invoking in the analytic sense that their conceptual unpacking calls for a reference to minds and their capabilities.

\*     \*     \*

The conception of a mind-invoking conceptual framework plays a central part in our articulation of conceptualistic idealism. But the sort of mental constructions at issue here have nothing private and idiosyncratic about them, quite to the contrary, they are a *social* creation. Categorial frameworks are not personal impressions of some sort; they inhere in conceptual schemes and the ground-rules for their deployment in language and other means of symbolic representation. We have to recognize the fundamentally public aspect of the means by which we construct our view of the world. Categorial frameworks are a social reality: they embody a shared conception of 'the way the world works.'

The conceptual machinery we deploy in shaping our view is neither imposed by objective features of a framework-neutral 'reality itself,' nor is it *innate* (i.e., wholly innate − fully determined by features of ourselves as human organisms). It is very largely a *cultural artifact*, socially formed and transmitted. Its features are not determined by the 'real world' itself − or rather are only partially determined by it. This means that it is interculturally variable and intraculturally changeable, and means also that we can learn about the framework and even (with great effort) deliberately change it.

The key point is that our idealism is not a mentalism that is in any way personal or idiosyncratic or subjectivistic. It insists that 'mind' is fundamental – but not an *individual* mind that contributes something personal and idiosyncratic. This idealism takes its stand on a publicly shared framework of concepts and ignores all that is subjective in terms of person-to-person variation. Its basis is language as enshrining conceptual scheme that is inherently interpersonal (unpersonal) and public. A *social* basis in a shared culture is the essential factor.

This view owes an obvious debt to Kant as regards the fundamentality of categories, but it rejects their Kantian inevitability and invariability. Our position holds that one cannot deal transcendentally at the level of generality of all possible frameworks because this leads to the same near-vacuity as a grammarian's attempt to deal with all possible languages or an economist's attempt to deal with all possible systems of exchange. (Thus our position acknowledges a debt to Ernst Cassirer's linguo-sociological neo-Kantianism.)

## 7. CONCEPTUAL IDEALISM

On the standard and traditional conception, idealism is the doctrine that things about which we can have knowledge, the *OBJECTS of knowledge*, depend in some essential way – perhaps in point of their very existence itself, but certainly as regards their nature as the sort of things they are – upon their being known, that is, upon their status as *objects OF KNOW-LEDGE*. Idealism, thus conceived, asserts a *relational* thesis, insisting on an unbreakable link between the ontological and the epistemological, between what exists on the one hand, and our knowledge of it on the other. On this broad conception, idealism is a generic thesis of which the historic doctrine of *material* idealism, maintaining the subordination of matter to mind, is only one specific instance – albeit perhaps the most important one.

Our present idealism sees the mental subordination or involvement at issue in neither *ontological* nor *epistemological*, but in *conceptual* terms. An *espistemological* mind-involvement is, of course, trivial: only minds, and beings possessed thereof, can have knowledge, entertain opinions, hold beliefs, etc. This truistic point is not at issue. Nor is our position of the traditional *ontological* type, holding that the material objects that all too evidently populate the physical world are only illusory and non-existent as such, but are mere 'works of the mind' (*entia rationis*). Rather, the present view maintains a *conceptual* idealism in holding that prime facets of natural objects *as we conceive of them* (and thus not necessarily as 'things in themselves' – whatever *that* might be) are such as to be construed, at least in certain respects, in terms whose adequate explication calls for a reference to minds and their capabilities.

The idealist position to be developed here addresses itself to certain key features of our common conception of things, viz., their particularity, spatiality, temporality and causality. These four items (space, time, material objects, and causality) must figure centrally in any discussion of idealism, and they will be a principal object of present consideration. Four corresponding theses lie at the hard-core of historical idealism to wit, the mind-dependency of space, time, material objects, and causality. The major figures of the idealist tradition all assume a position of emphatic mind-dependency with regard to these four items. Leibniz assigns all of them to the sphere of phenomenal appearance: they are phenomena (albeit well-founded phenomena) that are devoid of substantial reality. Kant accords all of them a transcendental – and so mind-dependent – status. For Bradley, while these items can and do play a decisive role in man's thought about things, none of them can have any sort of independent reality because a logical inconsistency is in each case involved (in ways that Bradley purports to demonstrate by intricate reasonings).

Our own discussion will also endeavor to argue for this sector of traditional idealist theory. The 'orthodox view' of the world conceives it in terms of particular things placed within space and time and interacting causally. The idealism that is espoused here maintains that each of these key features of our common conception of nature (viz., particularity, spatiality, temporality, and causality) are in the final analysis mind-involving in the conceptualistic manner this opening chapter has sought to clarify.

\*    \*    \*

Before embarking on the further development of such a conceptual idealism, some brief observations about the general strategy of argumentation are in order. The starting-point is to establish the mind-dependency of purely hypothetical possibilities, and then to argue that an appropriate explication of the conception of a 'law of nature' inherently involves recourse to hypothetical possibilities that also manifest lawfulness as mind-invoking. Proceeding beyond this point, it will be argued that the conceptions of causality, particularity, and space and time all involve an implicit reference to lawfulness which renders as mind-invoking this entire spectrum of concepts operative in the 'standard view of the world.'

As with the transcendental idealism of Kant, the pivot-point around which the theory revolves is presented by the modal aspect of necessity and possibility. With Kant, however, the leading issue was that of the origins of necessity, and his 'Copernican revolution' produced an idealism that sees mind as the origin of necessitation. With us, the key issue is that of the origins of possibility, and our theory sees the 'realm of possibility' as ultimately rooted in the operations of concept-deploying intelligence. Both these approaches are inevitably closely linked by the negation-duality obtaining between these modalities (necessary = not possible that not; possible = not necessary that not). And accordingly, a view which, like ours, sees possibility as mind-generated will ultimately also regard necessity as mind-imputed. But notwithstanding such a co-ordination of these two modalities from a *logical* standpoint, an approach based upon possibility is – as will be seen – significantly different in its *methodological* structure from one that is based upon a necessity-oriented point of departure along Kantian lines. At any rate, its stress upon the fundamentality and pervasiveness of the concept of the possible is a pivotal feature of the conceptual idealism these pages are concerned to articulate.

# Chapter II

# THE ONTOLOGY OF UNREALIZED POSSIBILITY: A CONCEPTUALISTIC THEORY OF THE MERELY POSSIBLE

## I. PRELIMINARIES

The sphere of the possible covers a wide range. There are the as yet unrealized possibilities that lie in the future. And there are the possible albeit unrealized doings of actual things, such as Smith's possible attendance at the film he failed to see last night, or the *dispositional* possibilities inherent in acorns and firecrackers. There are those things which are 'possible for all I know' – the *epistemic* possibilities, and many of these are as full-bloodedly real as anything can be – like the starters of a race, some among whom are 'possible winners' of it. But some states of affairs and some things are *merely* possible. They are not going to come to be realized in the future. Further inquiry is not going to have them turn out to be real. They are not simply alternative permutations of the actual. They are wholly unreal – *merely* possible in the most strictly hypothetical sense. These possible things and states of affairs which can possibly exist but actually don't – let us call them *hypothetical possibilities* – are paradigmatic of what I have in mind here in speaking of 'the possible.' These remote, totally actuality-detached possibilities will be central to the ensuing discussion.[1]

It deserves stress that those '*merely* possible' things and states of affairs which lie at the root of strictly hypothetical reasoning

[1] We are not at present concerned with impossibilities, since the question of their ontological status does not arise. To be sure they can be talked of, but this is an *empty* property: *anything* can be talked about. Now they not only fail to exist (in *any* sense of that term) but cannot in principle even be assumed or hypothesized to exist. They lack any sort of ontological basis: their standing here is not something small and tenuous, but literally zero. Thus the impossible does not concern us here, save insofar as 'possible'/'impossible' are contrast terms; rather, our present concern is with the contrast of the 'actual' with '(merely) possible.'

('suppose that there were an elephant on the front lawn') constitute the focus of consideration for the present chapter: the *purely hypothetical* possibilities as distinguished for those that are dispositional or epistemic or voluntaristically choice-dependent (the 'possible victim' of a robber), in all of which cases the possibility at issue is to be seen in terms of a *possibility for* some actually existing particular (for the actual runner to win this race; for the robber to fix upon that perfectly actual person).

The conception of 'nonentities' or 'unactualized possibles' or 'negative things' or 'unreal particulars' or 'nonexistent individuals' is among the most ancient and persistent notions in the history of philosophy. The fountainhead of subsequent discussions of nonexistent individuals is the philosophy of Parmenides as portrayed in the dialogues of Plato. In the *Sophist*[2] Plato espoused the Parmenidean view that all meaningful discourse (*logos*) must be *about a being* of some sort. Since winged horses and other nonexistent things can obviously be talked of meaningfully,[3] a rigid adherence to this doctrine would suggest for them a mode of being different from that of the *utterly* nonexistent which could not even be talked about or thought of. Plato did not hesitate to draw this consequence, and his view of these matters is the precursor of all treatments of the problem. A detailed survey of this sector of conceptual historiography could not fail to show the idea of nonexistent individuals to be historically respectable in its antecedents as well as to have substantial philosophical interest. We shall not, however, at present pursue

---

[2] See especially 236 E ff. 'It is also plain, that in speaking of something (*ti*) we speak of being (*ontos*), for to speak of an abstract something naked and isolated from all being is impossible' (*ibid.*, 237 D, tr. Jowett). Cf. also the discussion in the *Theaetetus*, 189 A.

[3] However, positive statements about nonexistents will presumably be false according to the correspondence theory of truth of *Sophist*, 261 E-263 B, since reality cannot provide the corresponding circumstances. Cf. Francis Cornford, *Plato's Theory of Knowledge* (New York, 1957), p. 212. But compare J. Xenakis' article 'Plato on Statement and Truth-Value, *Mind*, vol. 66 (1957), pp. 165–72, where it is argued that, for Plato, claims about nonexistents do not represent proper statements at all, and do not have a truth-value. However, see also the reply by J. M. E. Moravcsik, 'Mr. Xenakis on Truth and Meaning,' *ibid.*, vol. 67 (1958), pp. 533–7.

these historical byways further, referring the interested reader to a discussion given elsewhere.[4]

## 2. THE ONTOLOGICAL STATUS OF NONEXISTENT POSSIBLES

Putting aside historical observations, let us turn to the systematic issues. The central question can be posed in very old-fashioned terminology: What is the ontological status of nonexistent possibles? How, for example, can it be said without contradiction that 'there are' certain possibilities when it is said in the selfsame breath that these are *mere* possibilities, and so unreal and non-existent? In what manner do such possibilities have the being claimed for them when it is said that 'they are real possibilities,' when they *ex hypothesi* lack *real* being, i.e., existence?

Ontology – the theoretical study of the concepts revolving around such verbs as 'to be' or 'to exist' – is no mere logicians' game carried on for its abstract interest alone. And the ontology of possibility possesses a special importance: unless the problems that arise here are somehow clarified and resolved, one cannot get an adequate account of supposition and assumption. For in the absence of a workable theory of nonexistent possibles we could not have a satisfactory mechanism for the rational manipulation of such hypothetical inferences as: 'Assume the tiger in that cage were actually a unicorn; then . . .' And note that our concern is not with the existential status of the *proposition* 'that the unicorn is in the cage' (*qua* proposition), but rather relates to the existential status of the state of things that this proposition claims to obtain.

But just exactly what can the existential status of such possible-but-unrealized states of affairs possibly be? Clearly – *ex hypothesi* – the states of affairs or things at issue do not exist as such: only *actual* things or states of affairs can unqualifiedly be said to exist, and not those that are possible but unrealized. By definition, as it were, only the *actual* will ever exist in the world, and never the unactualized possible. For the world does not have two existential compartments, one including the actual and another that includes the unactual. Of course, unactualized possibilities can be conceived, entertained, hypothesized, assumed, etc. In this mode they do, in a way, exist – or 'subsist' if one prefers – not, of course, unqualifiedly in themselves, but in a *relativized* manner, as the objects of certain intellectual processes. But it goes without saying that if their ontological footing is to rest on *this* basis – or anything like it – then they are clearly mind-dependent.

This critical point that the realm of the hypothetical things is mind-dependent must be argued in detail. Note, to begin with, that in the actual-existence cases we have the prospect of a dualism. There is:

(1) The actually and objectively existing thing or state of affairs (e.g., with 'that dogs have tails' we have the tailed dogs) and

(2) The thought or entertainment or assertion of this thing or state of affairs.

But with nonexistent possibilities (e.g., horned horses) the ontological situation becomes monistic, because item (1) is clearly lacking, since the things in question just do not exist. And this difference is crucial. For in the dualistic actual-existence cases, (1) would remain even if (2) were done away with. But with nonexistent possibles there is (*ex hypothesi*) no items of category (1) to remain, and so category (2) is determinative. Exactly this is the basis of the ontological mind-dependence of nonexistent possibles.

In dealing with the *ontology* of the possible, our concern is not with the (very actual) *thought-of-the-possibility* but with the *possibility itself*, the (utterly non-existent) state of affairs that is thought of. We must distinguish clearly between these two items:

(i) the thought of the (nonexistent) possibility (*der Gedanke des Nichtseiendes*)

(ii) the (nonexistent) possibility thought of (*das nichtseiende Gedachte*)

When this distinction is duly observed, the 'ontological' aspect of the matter becomes quite clear:

(A) The ontological status *per se* of entry (ii), the (mere) possibility at issue, is simply zero: *ex hypothesi* the item at issue – the $X$ in view when we speak of 'the mere possibility that $X$' – does not exist at all.

(B) Clearly entry (i), the thought of the possibility, exists unproblematically in the manner of thoughts in general. And while its object (ii) does not 'exist' in reality, it does 'exist' (or 'subsist' or what have you) *as the object* of the thought.

(C) And then it becomes perfectly clear that *this* mode of 'being' – not as a reality but solely as an object of thought – is mind-dependent.

We come now to a purely conceptual point of some importance for the position being argued. A critical difference should be noted between successfully intentional mental processes such as *seeing* and *feeling* and pseudo-intentional mental processes like *assuming, supposing, hypothesizing,* etc. In both cases, the process, of course, has an *object* distinct from itself: in the case of seeing, *the actual cat* as it exists; and in the case of supposing, *the supposed cat* as I hypothesize it. Nevertheless, though an object of the mental process is present in both cases (seeing, supposing) the objectivity of these cases differs decisively. With *seeing* there is

(1) the cat-of-my-thoughts (as I envision it in full subjective panoply), and
(2) the *actual* cat *as it exists.*

With *supposing* there is

(1) the cat-of-my-thoughts (as I suppose it), and
(2) the *purported* cat *as I think of it.*

Now in the first case, that of seeing, there is a potential gap between the two terms. But this gap is *logically closed* in the second case, that of assuming or supposing, where the two items necessarily coincide. In the second case, unlike the first, *both* the 'subjective' and the 'objective' indications of the item at issue arrive necessarily at the selfsame terminus: no possible discrepancy can arise, because the only 'being' at issue in item (1) here is its being-for-thought. This is why a 'correspondence theory of truth' is otiose with respect to the latter: it is in principle impossible to have a mistaken conception of something one merely imagines, whereas with something real this is only too easy.

The case for the mind-dependency of mere (and so 'purely hypothetical') possibilities is obviously not based on any sort of empirical considerations as to the workings of minds, but is purely a matter of *a priori* conceptual analysis. There can be no unrealized possibilities somehow emplaced in the real and 'objective' world. All 'mere' possibilities are, as such, necessarily not real, but only to be imagined or supposed, etc., as real: they cannot be located but only *assumed* to be located, they cannot be handled, seen, heard, but only *supposed* to be handled, seen, heard. Of course, it is not a *property* of the imaginary dollar bill that it is not to be seen anywhere. Kant is quite right about this; the imaginary dollar bill is not to be imagined as an *invisible* dollar bill because we are as a matter of principle unable to see it (for then it would not be a dollar bill at all), but as one that is perfectly real – and so visible, handleable, etc. But although invisibility is *ex hypothesi* not a descriptive *property* that characterizes the imaginary dollar, it is all the same a regulative *fact* about it. It is not by way of their internal and thought-oriented properties, but by way of the external and reality-oriented facts about them that unrealized possibilities are mind-involving. (And these are not just contingent facts about the hypothetical, but necessary ones that serve to make the items at issue what they are.)

The argument for the mind-dependency of hypothetical possibilities thus proceeds as follows: The world of mind-independent reality comprises only the actual. This world does not contain a region where nonexistent or unactualized possibilities somehow 'exist.' Unactualized hypothetical possibilities *ex hypothesi* do not exist in the world of objective reality at all. Nor is it feasible to hold that unactualized possibilities exist in some mind-accessible 'Platonic' realm of (mind-independent) reality existing wholly outside the world-order of natural actuality. There goes the world of actual reality, buzzing along 'doing its own thing.' Unrealized reality does not and cannot form a part of it. Unactualized hypothetical possibilities lack an independent ontological footing in the sphere of objective reality: they can be said to 'exist' in only a subsidiary or dependent sense – that is, only insofar as they are *conceived* or *thought of* or *hypothesized* and the like. Their existence is confined to the intensional order – as the correlative objects of actual or possible thoughts (supposings, assumptions, hypotheses) *that something-or-other is so.* By hypothesis, the merely possible is unreal and does not form a constituent part of existential reality; the unreal is indeed *linked* to the real, but only obliquely through the assumptive processes that minds deploy in framing suppositions, hypotheses, and the like. The 'existence' of unreal possibilities is limited by their status as objects of mental acts, so that their existential status is mind-relative. For such a possibility, to be (*esse*) is therefore to be conceived (*concipi*) – or, rather, to be conceivable.[5] In consequence, unrealized possibility is mind-dependent in the strong, existential or *ontological* sense of the term.

This outline sketches the general strategy for holding that possibilities do not exist in some self-subsisting realm that is wholly 'independent of the mind.' The existential objectivity and autonomy of the real world does not underwrite that of the sphere of hypothetical possibility. Nature encompasses only the actual: the domain of the possible is the creation of intelligent organisms, and is a realm accessible to them alone. A 'robust realism of physical objects' is all very well, but it just will not plausibly extend into the area of the hypothetical. It can plausibly be contended that it would be foolish (or philosophically perverse) to deny the thesis: 'This (real) stone I am looking at would exist even if nobody ever saw it'; but one cannot reason by analogy to support the thesis: 'This nonexistent but possible stone I am thinking of would be there even if nobody could imagine it.'

One point of caution is immediately necessary. We are not saying that to be a possible (but unactualized) thing requires that this must *actually* be conceived (or entertained, hypothesized,

---

[5] To say this is not to drop the usual distinction between a thought and its object. If I imagine this orange to be an apple, I imagine it *as an apple* and not as an *imaginary* apple. But this does not gainsay the fact that the apple at issue *is* an imaginary apple that 'exists only in my imagination.'

etc.) – so as in fact to stand in relation to some *specific* mind. Rather, what is being said is that possible albeit unrealized states of affairs or things obtain an ontological footing – i.e., can be said to 'exist' in some appropriately qualified way – only insofar as it lies within the generic province of minds to conceive (or to entertain, hypothesize, etc.) them. Unlike 'actual' things that actually exist in their own right, unrealized possibilities exist only as objects of thought. Thus the ontological basis of 'merely' possible states of affairs is mind-involving in this generic sense, that the very concept at issue is only viable in terms of conceptions whose analysis demands reference to the workings of minds.

## 3. OBJECTIONS AND REPLIES

·It is crucial that our concern is not with assertions regarding or ideas about possibilities – which are obviously and trivially mind-involving – but with the possibilities themselves. I do not want to wander off into Bishop Berkeley's forest. For the present we are not concerned with the general idealist position that all substance – real and unreal alike – will in general require minds. We are prepared to recognize and admit the crucial distinction between the *attribution* of a property to an object by someone (which obviously requires a mind), and the *possession* of the property by the object (which is or may be presumed to be an 'objective,' mind-independent fact). But the purely hypothetical *mere* possibilities at issue here are inherently mind-related: the hypothetical cannot just 'objectively be' the case, but must be hypothesized, or imagined, or assumed, etc. Unlike real things, merely hypothetical ones lack, *ex hypothesi*, that objective foundation in the existential order which alone could render them independent of minds.

Of course, in a trivial sense everything that is discussed – real or unreal – bears *some* relationship to a mind. Unquestionably, no matter what truth *we* may think of is (*ex hypothesi*) such that *somebody* thinks of it, but what people think of is not the crux. Being thought of is not as such essential to the truthfulness of a truth. This whole way of approaching the matter – with reference to what 'is thought' to be the case – loses sight of our specifically focal issue of unrealized possibilities. Our position has no need for the (surely perverse) step of negating the distinction between a fact, say that the cat is on the mat (which could continue unaffected by a proscription of mind-invoking conceptions), and the thought or statement of a fact (which could not). As Kant rightly insisted, there is, after all, no *descriptive* difference *qua X* (yellow, cat-like, etc.) between an actual *X* and a possible one: the difference is wholly one of *ontological status*. The point is that the *condition* of (mere) possibility, unlike the *condition* of factuality, involves something (viz., a reference to the hypothetical) that would be infeasible in the face of a postulated absence of mind-involving conceptions.

But an objector might well protest as follows:

Your analysis views possibilities to be dependent upon minds and their conceptualizing capabilities in a manner in which actualities are not. But does not thought and language make *asserting* possible just as it makes *hypothesizing* possible, so that a removal of assertion would destroy the facts asserted just as much as a removal of supposition destroys the possibilities supposed. To remove minds from our frame of reference is also to remove the proper objects of all mental acts, be they actualistic or possibilistic in purport.

The flaw of this objection is highlighted by its final sentence. There is no adequate foundation for holding that actuality is in principle somehow created by its assertion: objectively real actuality may well be an object of assertion but is of its very nature not dependent upon it, having an independent existential basis. But the case of unactualized possibility is not analogous, since it lacks (*ex hypothesi*) just this 'independent' existential basis: unlike actualities, unactualized possibilities as such just do not exist in themselves. Actualities exist as such and can thus provide 'independently existing' objects, but with unrealized possibilities exactly this 'independently existing' object is lacking. Hypothetically possible but unactualized things and states of affairs by their very nature cannot 'objectively be' the case. Thus it just is not true that possibilities and actualities are correlative in such a manner that actuality, like possibility, is necessarily lacking in an amentalistic frame of reference.

Ours is thus a possibility-directed idealism. We do not follow arch-idealists – phenomenalists, for example – in their path towards maintaining that *actuality* is mind-involving. The phenomenalist maintains that anything real in nature is *wholly* analyzable in terms of actual and possible experiences.[6] We only hold that whatever is merely possible is analyzable in part (but an essential part) in terms of capabilities for patently mental acts like supposing, assuming, and the like.

Unrealized possibility is not something that one can meaningfully postulate objectively of a 'mindless' world – that is, a world from which all mind-involving conceptions have been abstracted. For if the hypothetical element (which is clearly accessible only in a world endowed with minds) were *aufgehoben* (annihilated), then whatever hinges on mental processes like supposition and assumption – specifically including possible things and states of affairs – would be *aufgehoben* too. Of course, *we* can think of an 'alternative possible world' that is unpopulated, and so mind-denuded, but yet endowed with unrealized possibilities – so long as we do not go so far as to abandon all invocation of the mentalistic sphere of the conceivable. But if one rigorously puts aside all invocation of minds and their capabilities, eliminating any and all reference to the mental, then the hypothetical element is lost, and unrealized possibility is lost with it.

We have no desire to be pushed to the extreme of saying that the 'being' of nonexistent 'possible beings' lies in their being actually *conceived*; rather, we take it to reside in their being *conceivable*.[7] The 'being' of an unactualized possibility does not

---

[6] J. S. Mill's famous thesis that matter is 'the permanent possibility of sensation' gains misleading aura of mind-independence when one focuses on 'permanent possibility' that is quite lost when one duly stresses the operative phrase 'of sensation.'

[7] Or 'conceivable subject to certain conditions' if genuine (e.g., physical) possibility is at issue. Note also that when the *possible* is coordinated with the *conceivable*, it is of course the *entire* range of possibility that is at issue, including both actualized and unactualized possibility: actual things are, of course, also conceivable. But *their* 'being' cannot (*ex hypothesi*) be said to reside in this alone.

inhere in its relation to this or that particular mind, but to its conceivability by mind-in-general, in terms of the linguistic resources that are a common capability of intelligence as we know it. This independence of any specific mind establishes the *objectivity* of nonexistent possibilities despite their mind-dependence. Just as an actual thing or state of affairs remains as such when not known, so an unactualized item is not affected if not conceived by any actual person. But this independence of specific minds does not render unactualized possibles independent of mind as such. Their mind-dependence is not a *particularistic* dependence upon a specific mind (as is that of a headache) but is *generic*: a dependence upon quintessentially mental processes and capabilities. (And, of course, generic mind-dependence is mind-dependence all the same.)

One further line of objection must be considered. Someone might protest as follows:

I grant that it makes sense to speak of possible nonexistent states of affairs, e.g., its being (merely) possible that a cat be on the mat. But such a *propositional* possibility posed by a that-clause surely does not give rise to possible *things*, and so does not justify us in speaking of *a* or *the* (nonexistent) cat on the mat. To speak of possible things or entities is to reify quite illegitimately the strictly propositional possibility that a thing-of-that-sort exists. But this substantizing move from a possible-that situation to the setting up of a *possible-thing* is highly problematic.

I largely endorse this objection, accepting it in all regards save one alone – viz., its claims to being an objection. Nothing we have said gainsays its complaint as to the queerness and dispensability of a realm of possible *entities* apart from their role in relation to that-theses. Throughout our discussion of ontology we have been careful to use such locutions as 'possibilities,' or 'possibles' or 'possible items.' The ontology of possibilities that has concerned us need not have a specifically thing-directed orientation in any entity-requiring sense; a possible thing is no more a species of thing an imitation bird-call is a bird-call. The existence-claims with which we are concerned are posed by locutions of the propositional variety typified by:

that-there-be-a-cat-on-the-mat

Nothing in this discussion requires us to invoke some queer entity, a possibilistic-cat, that is somehow in fact present upon the mat. The status of the 'existence' at issue in the thesis

It is (merely) possible that there be (exist) a cat on the mat.

is the target of our discussion, and not the being or existence of that queer entity, the *ex hypothesi* nonexistent cat that is mysteriously emplaced upon the mat. In the final analysis, it is the possibility of $X$'s, rather than the 'possible $X$'s' in question, with which we are concerned here.

The theory of nonexistent possibles, in the sense of *merely possible things*, is actually, as we see it, a somewhat misleading derivation from the conception of *unactualized states of affairs*, which is itself supervenient upon certain actualities. Thus the actual state of affairs:

(1) that there is no cat upon the mat

automatically gives rise (under appropriate conditions) to the following unactualized state of affairs

(2) that there should be a cat upon the mat.

And it is because of the status of (2) as a 'mere possibility' that one can appropriately speak of an unactualized possible entity such as

(3) the possible cat upon the mat

and in turn such more detailed (description-laden) variants as

(4) the possible Siamese tomcat upon the mat.

In the manner of this example, nonexistent particular things are in general parasitic upon unactualized states of affairs.[8]

---

[8] This section elaborates and develops some points made almost in passing in the section on 'Lawfulness as Mind-Dependent' in my book on *Scientific Explanation* (New York, 1970), pp. 113–21.

## 4. THE LINGUISTIC FOUNDATIONS OF UNREALIZED POSSIBILITIES

Among contemporary logicians, W. V. Quine especially has been concerned to attack the very idea of possible but nonexistent objects. Quine has assaulted this conception not only with weighty argument but also with amusing invective. In his influential paper 'On What There Is,' he has made great fun of possible nonexistent entities:

Take for instance, the possible fat man in that doorway; and, again, the possible bald man in that doorway. Are they the same possible man, or two possible men? How do we decide? How many possible men are there in that doorway? Are there more possible thin ones than fat ones? How many of them are alike? Or would their being alike make them one? Are no *two* possible things alike? Is this the same as saying that it is impossible for two things to be alike? Or, finally, is the concept of identity simply inapplicable to unactualized possibles? But what sense can be found in talking of entities which cannot meaningfully be said to be identical with themselves and distinct from one another.[9]

What Quine is after here is a principle of individuation (*principium individuationis*) for nonexistent yet possible items. But – his inclination to the contrary notwithstanding – this problem does not in fact pose any insuperable obstacles. Presumably a nonexistent possible is to be identified by means of a *defining description*. And on this, the classical aproach to the matter, the problems so amusingly posed by Quine encounter no decisive theoretical difficulties. How many possible (now *logically* possible) objects are there? Clearly as many as can be described distinctly – presumably an *infinite* number.[10] When are two possible objects identical? When their defining descriptions are 'logically identical'

---

[9] 'On What There Is,' *The Review of Metaphysics*, vol. 2 (1948), pp. 21–38; reprinted in L. Linsky (ed.), *Sematics and the Philosophy of Language* (Urbana, 1952), pp. 189–206. See pp. 23–4 (pp. 191–2 of the Linsky reprint). A cognate denial of nonexistent individuals and of the 'reality' of unrealized possibilities is found in J. M. E. McTaggart, *The Nature of Existence*, vol. 1 (Cambridge, Mass., 1921), bk 1, chap. 2.

[10] And, due to the existence parametrized descriptive terms (functors), there is presumably a nondenumerable infinity of them. But to say that they are all *possible* is not, of course, to say they are all *compossible*.

– that is, equivalent. The doctrine of possible objects entails no major logical anomalies. With nonexistents everything save existence alone (and its implications) remains precisely as with objects that 'really' exist, subject to one exception only: that existents can be differentiated by purely ostensive processes – pointing or other means of placement within 'this actual world' – whereas possibilities cannot be so indicated but must be differentiated by purely descriptive means, that is, by the descriptive indication of property-differences.

To say (as we have done) that the doctrine of nonexistent possibles poses no insuperable theoretical difficulties is not to deny that their introduction into our conceptual framework may complicate the logical situation somewhat. Here one consideration comes to mind primarily – one connected with their mode of individuation – namely their property-indeterminacy or inherent *descriptive incompleteness.*

With respect to any existent (i.e., actual existent) $x$ it will have to be the case that the following determinacy principle obtains:

(P) For any property $\phi$: If '$\phi x$' is false, then '$[\sim \phi]x$' is true, $\sim \phi$ being the property-complement of $\phi$ (i.e., $[\sim \phi]$ applies to something if $\phi$ does not).

This principle holds whenever $x$ is an actually existent object. Given any property whatsoever, a real thing either has this property, or else lacks it and so has its complementary property. Moreover, it holds whenever $x$ is a possible object described completely through its Leibnizian '*complete* individual notion,' for unlike the less recondite situation we envisage, Leibnizian possibilia are defined through their complete individual notions in such a way that for any such individual and any predicate $\phi$, either '$\phi x$' is true or '$[\sim \phi]x$' is true. But (P) will not hold for nonexistent possibles that are individuated – on the approach adopted here – through an identifying characterization that is descriptively incomplete. (When the incompleteness of $x$ is in point of $\phi$, neither $\phi$ nor $[\sim \phi]$ will hold of $x$.) Now to identify a nonexistent particular is to provide a description of it, and this description will in general have the feature of logical incompleteness: my carelessly discarded match might have started a fire in that forest, but we cannot say which trees were burned down in this possible fire. Unlike something real,[11] a mere possibility may be property-indeterminate: of the oak tree that might have grown from yonder recently crushed acorn we can say definitely neither that it is healthy nor that it is diseased: in point of health or disease this item remains altogether indeterminate. This inherent incompleteness of (non-Leibnizian) possibilia, serves to set them apart from paradigm (i.e., extant) things.

The essential role here of descriptive mechanisms indicates the indispensable part played in this connection by the descriptive instrumentalities of our language – its stock of adjectives, verbs, and adverbs. Now while these are doubtless tied to reality, the link to reality is attenuated when we move from universals to particulars and from their features to the things themselves. Once we have enough descriptive machinery to describe something real (e.g., to describe this pen, which is pointed, blue, 6 inches long, etc., etc.) we are *ipso facto* in a position to describe nonexistents (e.g., a pen in other respects like this one but 10 inches long). It is in principle impossible to design a language whose descriptive mechanisms suffice for discourse about real things alone, without affording the means for introducing nonexistents into discussion. The mechanisms of reference to nonexistents are an inherent linguistic feature. Any linguistic vehicle for communication adequate to a discussion of the real cannot but burst the bounds of reality when negation and denial come upon the scene.

Nonexistent possibilities thus have an amphibious ontological basis: they root in the capability of minds to perform certain operations – to describe and to hypothesize (assume, conjecture, suppose) – operations to which the use of *language* is essential, so that both thought processes and language enter the picture.[12]

---

[11] In the standard cases at any rate: in microphysics we may want to deny that a particle concurrently has *both* a definite momentum *and* a definite position.

[12] In this discussion we have taken a distinctly verbal (i.e., description-centered) view of unrealized possibilities. We have neglected, for example, the prospect of unreal things or states of affairs as presented quasi-visually (for example in hallucination). This is no serious deficiency because in such cases of illusion (rather than hypothesis) the mind-dependency aspect of the matter is all the more clear and non-controversial.

Their foothold in language is the factor that gives to unrealized possibilities the *objective* ontological basis which they undoubtedly possess. 'The possibility existed all right, only nobody thought of it at the time' is a perfectly viable locution whose import we might gloss as follows: 'The possibility "exists" as such because the means for its description exist, so that it can in principle be specified (individuated); the possibility *could* therefore in principle have been formulated, though in fact no one then hypothesized it.' And the statement, 'There are possibilities no one will ever conceive of' is also perfectly viable and can be glossed along analogous lines. Here actuality is prior to possibility (as Aristotle was wont to insist), but we must amend this by the thesis that the possibility-of-thing (i.e., entity-possibility) is posterior to the possibility-of-process (i.e., conceptual possibility). *It is the actuality of minds capable of deploying by way of hypotheses and assumptions the decriptive mechanisms of language that provides the ontological basis of nonexistent possibilities.* For such possibilities can be said to 'exist' only insofar as they are statable or describable in the context of their being supposed, assumed, posited, or the like.

Our view of the 'ontology' of the matter can now be put into brief compass. *Ex hypothesi*, whatever is an *unrealized possibility* does not 'exist' pure and simple. What exists are minds and their capabilities, and so, accordingly, also languages and their rules. Unrealized possibilities are *generated* by minds, and so can be said to 'exist' only in a secondary and dependent sense, as actual or potential objects of language-deploying thought. Such possibilities are the products of an *intellectual construction*. The ontological status of the possible is thus fundamentally mind-dependent, the domain of the possible being a mental construct. Accordingly, we arrive at a conceptualistic theory of the merely possible. It is not being said that something 'merely possible' cannot be 'a real possibility', but rather that its reality, such as it is, must be altogether mind-made.

Although we have taken a conceptualistic line in holding that mere possibilities are mind-involving, we do *not* want to say that this role of mind is a matter of individual volition and idiosyncratic whim. Though the reality of possibilities resides only in the mind's conception thereof, the critical fact remains that the mind proceeds in this constructive enterprise in a restricted and canalized way, by use of the structured and structuring framework of a conceptual scheme. The realm of the possible is a construct, but the construction is made with the perfectly real materials of the conceptual and theoretical mechanisms of the conceptual schemes we use in our description and rationalization of the real world about us.[13]

But consider the following line of objection which might be developed against this view:

> You say that minds generate possibilities (i.e., unrealized possibilities) through the use of language. Presumably, this means (*inter alia*) that possibilities are individuated as (purported) states of affairs corresponding to (certain) expressions of a language. Now for one thing, this makes possibility relative to specific languages. And further, how can the contrast between the possible and the impossible then be preserved at all? Given the open and developmental character of natural languages, there is – quite possibly – nothing sayable that a natural language can't say. Metaphor and the other ways of extending a language seemingly make the concept of 'the unsayable' a dubious one. (And if the only contrast one can get is between that which can only be said *easily* in a language and that which can only be said complexly, then the matter of the 'possibilities relative to the language' rests on a very shaky and unsatisfactory foundation.) Thus a conception of possibility in terms of the equation *possible* = *sayable* cannot have much discriminative bite to it.

Here the second part of the objection effectively answers the first: since, presumably, nothing sayable cannot in principle somehow be said in a language, the factor of language-relativity to *specific* languages is removed. And as regards the second argument, the contrast-objection, there is just no warrant for making the pair possible/impossible run parallel the pair sayable/

---

[13] For an ampler development of this constructive theory of possibility see Nicholas Rescher and Zane Parks, 'Possible Individuals, Trans-World Identity, and Quantified Modal Logic,' *Nous*, vol. 7 (1973).

unsayable. Even the impossible may well be described or stated, and need not be altogether ineffable. The key consideration is not that the impossible cannot be said, but that it cannot be said without in the final analysis espousing some sort of absurdity or contradiction: that it cannot correspond to a 'meaningful thought.' And just this essential correlation with 'meaningful thought' is the basis of the mind-dependence of the merely possible. To repeat: Unrealized possibilities are mind-dependent not because they can only be stated in language – that's trivial, *anything* can only be stated in language – but because they can only be said to 'exist' in a secondary and dependent sense, as the actual or potential objects of thought.

## 5. HISTORICAL RETROSPECT

Basically four positions have been held in the history of philosophy with respect to the ontology of mere, hard-core possibilities:

| Position | *This Position Bases the Ontological Status of Nonexistent Individuals in* | *Exponent* |
|---|---|---|
| Nominalism | language | Russell, Quine |
| Conceptualism | the mind | Stoics, Descartes, Kant, Brentano |
| Conceptualistic Realism | the mind of God | Some Scholastics. Leibniz |
| Realism | a realm of possibility existing independently of human language and thought | Plato, some Arabic Mu'tazilites, MacColl, Meinong |

Let us consider these positions from the angle of contemporary perspective. Regarded from this point of view, outright realism is not an attractive position. Present-day philosophers advisedly have a disinclination amounting to aversion toward postulating a Platonic realm of being that is distinct from the worlds of nature and of thought. Nor would Conceptualistic Realism nowadays be viewed as a viable position, for contemporary philosophers are unwilling to follow in the path of their predecessors (both before and after Descartes, Leibniz, and Berkeley) and obtain by theft – that is, by falling back upon theological considerations – what they believe ought to be the fruits of honest philosophical toil. Moreover, a *rigoristic* Conceptualism with reference to non-existent possibilities would not, I think, be regarded as an appealing position. For such a view must hold regarding nonexistent possibilities that *To be is to be conceived* – their *esse* is *concipi*. But the notion of *unthought-of-possibilities* is certainly too viable to be so easily dismissed. (Note that while 'it is possible though not conceived' is a perfectly viable locution, 'it is possible though not conceivable' is not viable, at any rate not in the *quasi-logical* rather than *psychological* sense of 'conceivability' that is relevant is our present discussion.[13] For our concern here is not with what people will in fact conceive, but with what is conceivable-in-principle.) And nonexistent possibilities would seem to have a solidity and objectivity of status that we hesitate to subject to the vagaries of what is and is not in fact thought of. We have our-selves preferred to move in the direction of going from 'to be *conceived*' to 'to be *conceivable*' – construing this in a broad sense that includes imaging and imagining. And once this approach has been purged of its psychological connotations, we have moved near to the nominalistic realm of what can be des-cribed and discussed, assumed and stated. Just here, in the sphere of linguo-centric considerations, we reach the ground which is at any rate most congenial to contemporary philosophers. The fashionably 'modern' view that the ultimate foundation for nonexistent individuals is linguistic (in a broadly functional and potentialistic rather than strictly actualistic manner) come close to returning in a full circle to the language-orientated conceptualism expounded in classical antiquity by the Stoics in their theory of *lekta* ('meanings'). The problem of nonexistent possibles once more illustrates the fundamental continuities of *philosophia perennis*.

[13] Regarding the issue of psychologism that arises here see chap. VIII of N. Rescher, *Essays in Philosophical Analysis* (Pittsburgh, 1969).

# Chapter III

# POSSIBILITY AS MIND-INVOLVING

## I. INTRODUCTION

Three significantly different sorts of possibilities must be distinguished as particularly relevant for present purposes:

(1) the *dispositional* possibilities of the actual (e.g., this acorn can grow into an oak). (Dispositional Possibility.)

(2) *counterfactual* possibilities which involve some hypothetical changes in the properties of actual things (*you* might also be here in this room in addition to myself, though you aren't). (Reality-modifying possibility.)

(3) *purely hypothetical* possibilities that call for more than mere rearrangements of the characteristics of the actual in dealing with altogether nonexistent things (there might be an elephant in the room – and, at that, not just one of the actually existing ones – though there isn't). (Novelty-introducing Possibility.)

So far our main concern has been with the third group. The preceding chapter has dealt with the *mere* possibilities that are altogether unreal. The discussion there of such 'mere' possibilities envisages items that do not exist at all: *utterly* nonexistent possibilities are at issue, rather than just the unrealized potentialities of something real. We did not adopt this focus there because hypothetical changes in the actual domain are not of interest or do not pose issues of equal seriousness; but rather because the problems they pose are of a variant, less reality-remote nature and call for a different line of approach, one to whose development the present chapter will be devoted.

The 'hypothetical' possibilities – merely possible but altogether nonexistent things and states thereof – have been argued above to be mind-dependent in the strong sense of their *ontological* mind-dependency. However, nothing follows from this regarding such 'softer' and less remote possibilities as the *possible but non-actualized* doings of actual things – the sorts of possibilities paradigmatically inherent in the dispositions, powers, and capabilities of the real. The present chapter proposes to extend the conclusion of the preceding discussion by arguing that *any* talk of unrealized possibilities is mind-involving, the less remote ones as well as those of the 'hard-core.' However – to put our cards on the table at the very outset – it will only be maintained that the mind-involvement operative with respect to such more 'realistic' possibilities is of the strictly *conceptual* mode; it being recognized that mind-dependency in the stronger, *ontological* manner in view in the preceding chapter is not now at issue.

## 2. THE MIND-INVOLVEMENT THESIS

All possibilistic claims regarding unrealized states of affairs have their principal point where the contrast between the actually real and the hypothetically possible is operative. To explicate adequately any locution like 'If . . . were so, which it isn't, then . . . would be the case' ultimately requires some reference to the essentiality hypothetical nature of the antecedent. But the conception of *unrealized possibility* is such that we cannot adequately explicate what is at issue without reference to supposings or assumings or the like. By their very nature, unrealized possibilities cannot exist as such, but must be thought of: they must presumably be hypothesized, or imagined, or assumed, or something of this sort. Unlike real facts, merely possible ones lack, *ex-hypothesi*, that independent foundation in the existential order which alone could render them free of all linkage to conceiving minds.[1]

---

[1] Of course some constructions of possibility are highly actualistic in orientation. For example, according to the theory of Megarian logicians, one on occasion espoused by Aristotle, we are to think that something is possible for an item of a certain type if it is actual for some item of that type (e.g., that it is possible that this oyster contains a pearl because some oysters do contain pearls). On this Aristotelian/Megarian theory, possibility (and accordingly necessity) becomes purely a matter of the circumstances of the actual, and accordingly such possibilities secure a wholly sufficient foothold in the existential realm, and can consequently be constructed as mind-independent. But, for this very reason, these are not, of course, instances of the sort of genuinely hypothetical possibilities that are at issue in our discussion.

What is being said when – for example – one speaks of the (unrealized) potentialities of actual things? Whatever it is, it is clearly to be framed by a *hypothetical* proposition. When we say that this dried-up acorn had the potential of developing into an oak we mean something like this, that *if* adequate water had been forthcoming, and other suitable conditions fulfilled, *then* the acorn would have grown into an oak. The paradigm of such potentiality-claims is that, given the way things work in the world (or some relevant sector of it), then, subject to a certain *assumption or hypothesis or supposition* (viz., the availability of adequate water, etc.), some result must be accepted as ensuing (viz., the development of the acorn into an oak). The very formula in which the potentiality-claim is to be explicated couches it in mind-invoking terms (of suppositions and acceptances). Every hypothetical claim requires us to refer to some supposition or its consequences. ('Suppose there were an elephant in the room; then . . .,' or 'If there were an elephant in the room, then there would be a pachyderm in the building.')

Of course, a possibilistic claim, such as 'This lump of sugar is soluble,' does not generally talk about minds but something else (the sugar). But all the same, what it *says* about the sugar, viz., that it will dissolve 'in certain circumstances,' i.e., that *if* certain circumstances were realized – which they are not but may be assumed to be – then certain results must (be supposed to) obtain, is something that is framed in mind-referring terms of reference. It is not in employing such characterizations we fail to say 'what nature is in fact like.' Rather we say what *the real facts* are in *terms of reference* that are mind-involving. Such conceptual 'mind-dependency' does not conflict either with the factual correctness nor even with the 'reality' of the claims made. It simply means that we have presented what is held to be 'really and factually' the case from a mind-invoking conceptual perspective, in that the very terms of reference we employ are mind-invoking.

There is not and cannot be any 'objective,' mind-independent mode of iffiness in nature: objective states of affairs must be categorical, they cannot be hypothetical (or – for that matter – disjunctive) in the final analysis. The introduction of the hypothetical mode requires – i.e., *conceptually requires* – reference to the mentalistic capabilities of assuming, supposing, or the like. Any careful analysis of possibility inevitably carries one back to the common theme that only the actual can objectively be real, and that the modally variant areas of the possible and necessary depend essentially upon an invocation of mentalistic capacities. Applicability of the conception of unrealized possibilities demands recourse to the patently mind-invoking resources of hypothesis and supposition, which alone afford a footing for the sphere of the inexistent.

To motivate the important perspective at issue here, we must examine more closely the nature of the if-then thesis inherent in claims like 'If this button is pressed, the bell will ring.' Such a claim has two components: (1) the actualistic thesis that whenever an occasion of the button's being pressed is actually at hand, the bell does ring, and (2) actuality-transcending thesis that even when the button is not in fact pressed, still if it *were* the case that the button be pressed on such an occasion (which it by hypothesis is not), then the bell's ringing would also be the case. Now it is clear that only the first of these theses relates to the actual occurrences of the world's history, and that the second goes outside the sphere of actual occurrences, in hinging upon the 'merely hypothetical circumstance' of a *conditio irrealis* that is not part of reality at all. The realm of what exists in nature includes only what is real and actual; and it is altogether determinate, excluding the indeterminacy of anything 'merely possible'. Any suitably general if-then thesis is reality-transcendent and carries us into the sphere of hypothetical possibility. Reality is invariably categorical and actualistic, never iffy and hypothetical: it embraces only what actually exists and not any mode or manner of unrealized circumstances. To say that something is real is by this very fact to characterize it as actual and not hypothetical.

Of course, any generic statement of a natural law ('Sugar is water-soluble') or any specific attribution of a dispositional property ('That iron crescent is magnetized') is reality-transcending in underwriting of if-then thesis of fact-transcending import. And any articulation of a scientific or common-sense view of nature that is to underwrite hypothetical and assumptive reasoning will be replete with such claims whose force is fact-transcending. But to say this is to grant that our description of 'the real world' is given fact-transcending terms.

And not just 'fact-transcending', but even mind-invoking. If a conditional of 'if-then' form is to have actuality-transcending force, then its explication demands a suppositional analysis ('Assuming the antecedent condition – in the context of a suitably supplementary circumstance – the consequent follows'). We arrive at a suppositional theory of possibility: 'merely logical' possibility is basic, and all other modes of possibility revolve about the issue of what is logically possible *in context* (i.e., under given stipulations of the surrounding facts).

There is clearly an absolute gulf fixed between reality and irreality, between the actual and the 'merely possible.' Our theory has it that this gulf can be crossed only by mental acts of assumption and supposition. The only entry-point into the realm of the unreal is via a *mind*, capable of essentially imaginative processes like assuming, supposing, and the like. And this fact renders possibility as intrinsically mind-invoking – even the 'natural possibility' inherent in the dispositional functioning of the real.

The line of argument we have been taking may be summarized as follows:

(1) Possibility-talk is pointful only where the prospect of unrealized states of affairs is held in view.

(2) Unrealized states of affairs cannot be introduced upon the stage of consideration in any ostensive way; they must be introduced by way of assumption or hypothesis.

(3) This fact that the introduction of possibilities upon the stage of consideration calls for reference to some mind-involving capability renders the idea of possibility itself as conceptually mind-invoking (in our standard sense that a full-dress analysis of the meaning of this concept and its conditions of applicability ultimately drives one into making some reference to minds and their capabilities). Accordingly,

(4) All possibility is mind-involving, the purely hypothetical in the more existentially laden sense of this term, the rest

in the conceptual mode of mind-invocation that is central to the present theory.

### 3. SOME OBJECTIONS

Consider the following objection:

> Let us begin with the point – you do not hesitate to grant it – that whatever there is about the 'real world' that verifies assertions doubtless does much else beside, and does so whether or not there is any asserting going on in the universe. But is it not equally true that there are possibilities existing independently of any and all mental activities of supposing? Take, for example, the possibility that this acorn the squirrel is now eating will grow into an oak tree. This is an unrealized possibility, to be sure, but it is certainly subject to and indeed derivative from constraints regarding the functioning of the real. For it is clearly proper to say 'Acorns *can* grow into oak trees (even when they do not), while peanuts cannot.' Surely what acorns potentially *can* do is subject to constraints inherent in the nature of the real, constraints of the same character as those governing what they in fact *do* do. And such possibilities are surely independent of any supposing that may or may not be done.

Now nobody wants to deny (or at any rate I do not) that there is a perfectly good sense of 'possibility – namely one articulated with reference to 'the potentiality of the natural development of actual things' – in which acorns may possibly develop into oak trees and peanuts not. But the very nature of this possibility, like any other, is revealed by its conceptual unraveling to depend critically upon theses of the 'what-would-happen-if' type. This claim is that: 'Actual, *objective* reality (and this does and must come in explicitly) is such that if certain conditions were to be met then certain results would ensue.' And just this essential reference to the consequences of the (*ex hypothesi* unrealized) meeting of 'certain unactualized conditions' introduces a suppositional factor into the 'objective' characterization of the properties of the acorn, so as to reveal this characterization as itself built

E

up in mind-invoking terms. It merits reemphasis that the mind-dependency in view pertains strictly to the *conceptual* order. It is a matter of finding an implicit reference to minds in the analytical unpacking of the concepts at issue in what is being said. The key fact is that in the final analysis the iffiness of any possibilistic talk invokes 'what would happen if' and so carries back to the mind-referring area of what can be supposed, hypothesized, assumed or the like.[2]

Thus to a question like 'why should not the malleability of this lump of lead be every bit as real or objective as its shape or mass seemingly are?' we reply: 'The issue is not one of *reality* at all, but *objectivity* – if this 'objectivity' be construed as independence of any and all mentalistic aspect. Malleability is not just a matter of what the lead does, but of *what it would do if*, and this introduces a suppositional or hypothetical element which can only be explicated in mind-invoking terms.' No doubt the lead has the mind-invoking dispositional feature of malleability as a causal consequence of something it objectively and mind-independently *is*: its potentiality roots in its actuality – its 'can-dos' are ultimately grounded in its 'ises.' But the very conceptual nature of potentiality rules out the prospect of viewing 'objectively real possibility' as independent of any and all mind-invoking references, overt or covert, to the sphere of 'what might be if.'

An objector may ask: 'But why should we not say that there *really are* possibilities which determine the truth of possibility-claims just as there really are actualities determining the truth of actuality-claims?' To this one can but reply as follows: First off, we grant that the *existence* of the actualities at issue is unproblematic, since the 'really is' of an actuality resides simply and straightforwardly in its existence. But this concession leads to the question: How could one conceivably construe the 'really is' of

---

[2] Of course, even purely factual theses generate hypothetical consequences: e.g., if *a* has $\phi$, then clearly 'If something has $\phi$, then it shares at least one property with *a*.' But its having some mind-involving consequence is not sufficient to establish the mind-involvingness of the thesis at issue, any more than its having some hypothetical consequences prevents a categorical thesis from being categorical. The operative issue is that of the analytical make-up of the thesis itself.

the unrealized possibility in a parallel way, where the equation 'really is' = 'actually exists' is *ex hypothesi* broken? The 'really is' of an unrealized possibility is intelligible only in hypothetical terms – with reference to suppositions and their consequences – and accordingly introduces an ineradicably mind-invoking perspective.

Moreover, the previous objection misses contact with the *conceptual* idealism here at issue. To say that a reality is presented in mind-invoking terms is not to deny it its claims to being real, or to maintain that it is somehow a 'mere fiction.'

Another possible objection must be dealt with:

Your analysis of (unrealized) possibility in terms of suppositions and hypotheses is surely deficient. Anything that is *logically* possible may be supposed, but some things are actually possible and others not. Your approach avoids the issue of the truth or the reality of the possibility at issue. An acorn can properly be supposed to develop into an oak tree (even should it fail) but a peanut not.

This objection overlooks the crucial issue of the *background or context* of a supposition. Any discussion of what is possible proceeds against the background of a substantial body of continued and unaltered rational commitments – some view as to the fundamental facts regarding how things work in nature. Given that I want to retain the sizes of things, I cannot assume that there are 10,000 people in this room. Given that I want to retain *the basic facts as to how things work in the world*, I cannot assume peanuts develop into oak trees. The difference between 'real' and 'merely speculative' possibilities does *not* turn on the fact that the latter are suppositional and the former not; *both* are in fact suppositional, although different contexts of background or frame of reference are operative with respect to the suppositions in the two cases.

Our approach does not obliterate the distinction between different types of possibility (e.g., near and remote), but prepares the ground for it. In the context of fixed invariants in the 'background,' some assumptions will obviously be blocked. And insofar as our standard conceptual scheme for viewing natural reality has a whole cluster of rather fundamental commitments, there will, of course, be many possibilities that one will have to dismiss as 'merely speculative' and unable to qualify as 'genuine possibilities.'

Our approach might be characterized as that of a *compatibility theory of possibility*: the logically possible is that which is compatible with itself; and all other modes of possibility (physical possibility, technical possibility, etc.) are matters of compatibility with some coordinated context of 'background' stipulations (laws of nature, the technology of the time, etc.). We do not deny the existence of such significantly diverse modes of possibility as the 'purely speculative' and the 'natural,' but insist that because of their essentially hypothesis-invoking character, all of these types rest on assumptions, suppositions, etc., in such a way as to introduce the characteristic capabilities of minds upon the stage of consideration.

## 4. THE 'MIND-DEPENDENCY' AT ISSUE IS CONCEPTUAL

It cannot be overemphasized that the mode of mind-invocation at issue in our thesis regarding the 'mind-dependency' of possibility is strictly conceptualistic. Thus, consider the objection that – 'Surely it was possible before there were any minds in the universe that there should be minds; hence possibilities antedate minds and are accordingly not mind-dependent.' This objection misses its target if aimed at our position. Its entire approach is altogether misleading. Our present preoccupation is not with a point of conjectural natural history, but is strictly *conceptual* in character. The conceptual unraveling of the idea of 'hypothetical possibilities' demands deployment of mind-related conceptions. Thus the dependence at issue is conceptual and not causal. We are certainly not saying that the 'real world' (the extra-mental world – whatever it is) somehow becomes different with the introduction of minds. The whole issue of historico-causal dependencies is entirely beside the point, and even to talk of a mental *creation* of possibility is to set up something of a straw man. Let it be granted – by way of analogy – that there were colors (in the sense of phenomenal colors) in the universe long before there were any sight-endowed beings; this in no way prevents phenomenal color from being *conceptually* sight-referring, e.g., that orange is the color a visually normal person sees when looking at an orange under normal conditions of lighting, etc. In fine, it is a *conceptual* dependency upon mind-referring notions rather than any *causal* dependency upon the functionings of minds that is at issue in our discussion. The mind-involvement of a 'real' possibility is not in the *ontological* order, like that of a headache.

The following objection against the conceptualistic theory of possibility could also be attempted:

> If possibility is (as your analysis has it) somehow mind-involving, then the extra-mental world is devoid of potentiality. It then seems that there are no longer *contingent* events in (extra-mental) nature – events possibly other than what they actually are. But then one can no longer distinguish between what is actual and what is necessary, and we are driven to the fatalistic result that whatever happens must happen.[3]

But this objection will not stand. Our analysis does not show that actuality and necessity somehow *coincide* in the sphere of mind-independent reality (so that whatever is actual here is also necessary). It shows that the entire distinction possible/actual/necessary is (categorially inoperative in this sphere as a *distinction*, because *in principle* only the actual can (virtually *ex hypothesi*) exist simply and as such. No fatalistic result ensues from this, however. Although the sphere of altogether mind-independent reality includes only the actual – and no 'unrealized possibilities' can exist within it – it does not follow that what belongs to this sphere belongs to it of necessity. To claim this would be to confuse the necessity of consequence with absolute necessity, because being a consequence of the *ex hypothesi* actual with a necessity relativized to this actuality is certainly not tantamount to necessity pure and simple.

To say that the conception of alternative possibilities is mind-invoking is not to say that these possibilities are unreal in the

---

[3] Cf. Lee C. Rice, review of *Essays in Honor of Carl G. Hempel*, ed. by N. Rescher *et al.*, *The Modern Schoolman*, vol. 48 (1971), pp. 179–81 (see p. 181).

sense of improper (let alone impossible). It is a matter of the angle from which we take our perspective. *Within* the standard framework of our concepts possibilities need have no specifically mentalistic involvements: there is no *further* element of 'mind-dependency' over and above what we paid by way of an entrance fee. But the *external* fact remains that this framework is articulated in terms of conceptually mind-involving terms of reference. And, of course, it does not follow that these mind-invoking conceptions are in any way unreal or inapplicable·

## 5. A PROBLEM OF CIRCULARITY

Does one not reason in some sort of a circle in saying that possibility is ultimately to be construed in terms of conceivability, something which in turn requires reference to the possible – to what *can be conceived*? Isn't the specification of possibility-in-general in terms of mentalistic possibilities a nonproductive circumambulation? Not really. For our position is not circular but reductive: its stance is that *all* possibility is in the final analysis inherent in and derivative from mental possibility. We maintain that the reality of unrealized, *merely possible* states of affairs is dependent upon the reality of the possibility-involving processes of actual things (viz., mind-endowed beings) through the *construction* of descriptions, and the hypothesizing (assuming, postulating) of their existence. We are saying that when the-possibility-of-the-thing is its only 'reality' then this 'reality' inheres in a possibilistic intellectual process. Here actuality is indeed prior to possibility – the actuality of one category of things (viz., minds with their characteristic modes of functioning) underwrites the *construction* of the totality of nonexistent possibles. Consequently, *substantive* possibility, the possibility of altogether hypothetical unrealized states of affairs and things, is conceptually consequent upon *functional* possibility, the possibility inherent in the 'can do' of processes and capabilities – specifically mentalistic ones. And at this stage we arrive at mind-involvement of an overt and blatant sort.

Intellectual possibilities are thus seen as being fundamental: the basic category of possibilities comprises possible *descriptions* – language-enshrined concepts – and so involves items that are in substantial measure linguistic in nature (construing language in the broad sense of the symbolic process in general). Accordingly, whatever 'being' or 'quasi-reality' nonexistent possibilities have is consequent upon the actuality of minds and their modes of functioning, for it is based upon and derivative from the real functional potentiality of mental processes: the mental capacities for assuming, supposing, and the like. In affording the mechanisms of conceivability, minds come to be functionally operative in such a way as to render the whole range of unrealized possibility as such mind-involving. On this view, the fundamentality of mentalistic possibility is the locus of the mind-invocation of possibility in general.

# Chapter IV

# LAWFULNESS AS MIND-INVOLVING

## 1. WHAT IS A UNIVERSAL LAW?
### THE NATURE OF LAWFULNESS

Scientific explanations of the circumstances and occurrences of nature are subsumptive arguments: they position particular events and states of affairs as special cases within a systematic framework of order delineated through laws. Our standard concept of explanation – causal explanation preeminently included – is such as to require that the generalizations used for explanatory purposes must be of a special sort: they must be *lawful*.[1] And clearly, not just any universal empirical generalization will qualify as a law in this scientific context of discussion – no matter how well established it may be. It is critically important to distinguish here between *accidentally true* generalizations on the one hand and *lawful* generalizations on the other. 'All coins in my pocket weigh less than one ounce' and 'All American presidents are native of the *continental* United States' are examples of accidentally true generalizations. By contrast, generalizations like 'All elm trees are deciduous,' 'All (pure) water freezes at 32° F' and 'All Y-chromosomes self-duplicate under suitable stimulation' are lawful. A (potentially accidental) generalization can as such claim merely that something *is* so, perhaps even that it *is always* so; a lawful generalization goes beyond such a merely *de facto* claim to stipulate that something *must* (in some appropriate sense) be so.

Thus consider the following two explanatory answers to the question: 'Why did that tree shed its leaves last fall?'

(1) Because it is an elm, and *all elms are deciduous*.

---

[1] The analysis of explanation and lawfulness given in this chapter was initially presented in the author's *Scientific Explanation* (New York, 1970). The present discussion is indebted to the treatment given there, though representing a substantial expansion of, and, hopefully, improvement upon it.

(2) Because it is a tree on Smith's property, and *all trees on Smith's property are deciduous.*

The drastic difference in the satisfactoriness of these two 'explanations' is due exactly to the fact that the generalization deployed in the first case is lawful, whereas that in the second is not.

Natural laws are akin to but significantly different from both rules and descriptions. Like rules, laws tell us how things 'must be,' yet unlike most familiar rules laws admit no exceptions, but are always 'obeyed.' Like descriptions, laws state how things are; yet unlike standard descriptions, laws go beyond describing how things in fact *are* to make claims about how they *must be.* Thus laws are akin both to descriptive characterizations and to norms; they have both a descriptive and a rulish side that prevents their being grouped squarely into either category. And the nomic aspect inherent in their rulishness is the essential feature that marks them as genuine laws.[2]

But just what is this factor of lawfulness present with respect to some generalizations and absent with others? The best way to answer this question of what lawfulness *is* is by inquiring into what it *does.* Lawfulness manifests itself in two related ways: *nomic necessity* and *hypothetical force.* Nomic necessity represents the element of *must*, of inevitability. In asserting it *as a law* that 'All A's are B's' ('All timber wolves are carnivorous') we claim that *it is necessary* the world being as it is, that an $A$ will be a $B$ (i.e., that a timber wolf will under appropriate circumstances unfailingly develop as a meat-eating animal).

This nomic necessity manifests itself most strikingly in the context of hypothetical suppositions – with counterfactual hypotheses especially. In accepting the contention that 'All $A$'s are $B$'s (All spiders are eight-legged') *as a law*, we have to be prepared to accept the conditional 'If $x$ were an $A$, then $x$ would be a $B$.' ('If this beetle were a spider [which it is not], then it would have eight legs.' 'If the [nonexistent] animal I'm thinking of were a [real]

---

[2] This nomological necessity of laws is generally called 'nomic necessity,' following W. E. Johnson, *Logic, Part III* (Cambridge, 1924), p. 9. Cf. J. M. Keynes, *A Treatise of Probability* (London, 1921), pp. 251 and 263 where Keynes speaks (*pace* Hume) of the lawfulness of general uniformity as involving a 'necessary connection.'

spider, then it would have eight legs.')[3] It is preeminently this element of hypothetical force that distinguishes a genuinely lawful generalization from an accidental generalization like 'All coins in my pocket weigh less than one half ounce.' For we would not be prepared to accept the conditional 'If a Venetian florin were in my pocket, then it would weigh less than one half ounce.'[4] The critical difference between a merely factual (and so potentially accidental) generalization and an authentically lawful one does not reside in the reference to a specific particular (why could a law not be particular-pertaining, as, for example, a personality trait is with humans) nor in reference to a limited period of time (why could a law not obtain during one transient cosmic era?). Rather, the critical aspect of a law lies in the force of necessity it carries. And on this, surely most plausible conception of lawfulness, there is no reason of principle why a genuinely lawful relationship could not obtain with respect to one particular thing (the magnetic north pole or the Van Allen radiation belt) or one particular spatio-temporal region (a black hole).

The fact is that the statement

(I) All X's are Y's

makes a stronger claim when put forward as a law than when put forward as a 'mere' generalization. For if (I) is construed as a law, then it asserts 'All X's have to be Y's,' and so we obtain the stronger nomological generalization:

---

[3] The double example has a point: the $x$ of the formula ranges over existents and nonexistents alike. In the former case (when we assume an actually existing thing to be different) we have a *modificatory counterfactual* conditional whose antecedent negates some actual fact. ('If this dog in the room were an elephant [which it isn't], then . . .') In the second case (when the thing at issue is nonexistent) we have a *speculative* counterfactual. ('If there were an elephant in the room [which there isn't], then . . .') The former type *changes* the things of this actual world, the latter type makes additions to (or subtractions from) them. It will not be without significance for our subsequent argument that laws support counterfactuals of both the actuality-modifying and the novelty-introducing varieties.

[4] It is clear that we mean this to be construed as 'if it were somehow *added to* the coins in my pocket' and not as 'if it were to be somehow *identical with* one of the coins in my pocket.'

(II) All X's are Y's *and further* if any z that is not an X were an X, then z would be a Y.[5]

When a generalization is taken as lawful it obtains added force: it gains a further assertive increment – even though this nomic necessity will express itself primarily in applications of a counter-factual or fictional kind. It is in the conceptual nature of things that nomic necessity manifests itself most strikingly in such hypo-thetical and counterfactual contexts.[6]

To clarify this nomic-necessity aspect of lawfulness let us con-sider the counterfactual supposition: *Assume that this wire (which is actually made of copper) were made of rubber.* This supposition occurs in the following context:

*Items of Knowledge*
Facts: (1) This wire is made of copper.
   (2) This wire is not made of rubber.
   (3) This wire conducts electricity.
Laws: (4) Copper conducts electricity.
   (5) Rubber does not conduct electricity.
Hypothesis: Not-(2), i.e., This wire is made of rubber.

[5] Roderick M. Chisholm has put this point with admirable precision: 'Both law statements and non-law statements may be expressed in the general form "For every *x*, if *x* is an S, *x* is a P." Law statements, unlike non-law statements, seem however to warrant inference to statements of the form, "If *a*, which is not S, were S, *a* would be P" and "For every *x*, if *x* were S, *x* would be P".' R. M. Chisholm, 'Law Statements and Counterfactual Inference,' *Analysis*, vol. 15 (1955), p. 97. Any such for-mulation plainly leaves open the question of whether the variable '*x*' at issue ranges over *actualia* only, or mere *possibilia* as well.

[6] Of course strictly factual statements also underwrite counterfactuals. From 'Mr. X has property $\phi$' it (presumably) follows that 'If Mr Y were Mr X, he would have property $\phi$.' But note that it is a relationship of *identity* that is at issue here. When I use the law 'copper conducts electricity' to infer 'If this stick were copper, it would conduct electri-city' this is not to be construed in identity terms as 'If this stick were to be identical with one of the existing copper objects it would conduct electricity' but rather as 'If this stick were somehow added to the exist-ing copper objects, it would conduct electricity.' Thus the counterfactual claims at issue in the discussion must be construed as other than mere suppositions of reidentification.

To restore consistency in our knowledge in the face of this hypothesis we must obviously give up (1) and (2). But this is not sufficient. One of (5) or (3) must also go, so that *prima facie* we could adopt either of the conditionals:

(A) If this (copper) wire were made of rubber then it would not conduct electricity (because rubber does not conduct electricity).

(B) If this (copper) wire were made of rubber, then rubber would conduct electricity (because this wire conducts electricity).

That is, we get a choice between retaining (5) with alternative (A) and retaining (3) with alternative (B). In classing a generalization as a 'law' we undertake an epistemic commitment to retain it in the face of counterfactual hypotheses in such a manner that the conditional (A), viz., 'If this wire were made of rubber then it would not conduct electricity' strikes us as natural *vis-à-vis* (B).[7] To treat a generalization as a law is to endow it with a status of inevitability – of (relative) necessity – that gives it priority in cases of this sort.

Yet another effective way to motivate the distinction between a 'law' and a 'mere generalization' is to consider the effect of contraposition.[8] The fact is that the statement

(1) All X's are Y's

makes a stronger claim when put forward as a law than when put forward as 'mere' generalization. For if (1) is construed as a law it asserts 'All X's *have to be* Y's,' that is, we obtain the stronger *nomological* generalization:

(1a) All X's are Y's *and further* if any $z$ that is not an X were an X, then $z$ would be a Y.

When a generalization of the type (1) is taken in this nomological way, then contraposition will fail. For

[7] The considerations at issue here are treated in more detail in my book on *Hypothetical Reasoning* (Amsterdam, 1965).

[8] For a more detailed and elaborate treatment of the problem of law-contraposition see N. Rescher, 'Counterfactual Hypothesis, Laws, and Dispositions,' *Nous*, vol. 5 (1971), pp. 157–78.

(2) All non-Y's are non-X's

when construed as stating a law, asserts:

(2a) All non-Y's are non-X's *and further* if any $z$ that is not a non-Y were a non-Y, then $z$ would be a non-X.

Although the generalizations (1) and (2) are equivalent, this is not the case with their nomological counterparts (1a) and (2a). These statements are nonequivalent since, *inter alia*, (1a) stipulates that the $z$ at issue in it is to be a non-X, while (2a) stipulates that the $z$ at issue in it is to be a Y (and neither statement justifies relating non-X's and Y's). Thus *seemingly equivalent generalizations can formulate different, nonequivalent laws.* When a generalization is taken as nomological, that is, as stating a law, it obtains an assertive increment (albeit one of a strictly counterfactual sort) of such kind that contraposed – and so *seemingly* equivalent – generalizations need no longer represent the same law.[9]

It is thus built into our very concept of a law of nature that such a law must – if it be of the universal type – correspond to a universal generalization claimed to possess nomic necessity and denied to be of a possibly merely accidental status. Even if the generalization were claimed to hold *in fact* for all places and times, even this would not of itself suffice for lawfulness: it would still not be a law if its operative effectiveness were not also extended into the hypothetical sphere. The conception of a universal law operative in our standard concept of scientific explanation is thus very complex and demanding. A generalization of lawful status goes beyond the purely actualistic claims of a merely factual generalization as such: it involves claims not only about the realm of observed fact, but about that of hypothetical counterfact as well. On our standard conception of the matter, a generalization just *is not lawful* if it does not apply to *all* instances, actual and possible, real and purely hypothetical alike. A thesis that is put forward as a genuine law thereby purports to pertain not only to things and states of affairs as they stand, but

---

[9] The issues revolving around this point have been analyzed in greater detail in 'Counterfactual Hypotheses, Laws, and Dispositions' (*op. cit.*).

also to their dispositional and hypothetical variants. Otherwise the indispensable usefulness of laws in contexts of hypothetical reasoning could be destroyed, for we could not use laws to reason from fact-contravening suppositions as in fact we readily do. Just these far-reaching claims are indispensable to the acceptance of a generalization as lawful and represent a formative constituent of our standard conception of a universal law of nature.

The prospect of hypothetical applications is a crucial facet of the lawfulness of law-theses. A thesis describing the fall of objects only on specific actual occasions, without any implicit claims as to their behavior 'under certain circumstances,' could hardly qualify as a *law of nature*, as this is and always has been understood. Laws do not merely serve to explain actual occurrences but enable us to reason about their possibilistic variants as well (and indeed they serve to determine the sphere of what is physically or nomically possible). Thus Galileo's law of falling bodies not only accounts for the fact that this stone has dropped five feet since its release for free fall *in vacuo*, but enables us to say what would have happened if its release had occurred one second earlier, and even to say what would have happened if we had released some other, purely imaginary stone in its place.

The two sectors of irreality – the reality-modifying and the novelty-introducing – stand on a very different footing as regards lawfulness. It might well be argued that the application of laws in relation to merely possible and altogether inexistent things might be viewed as an incidental or somehow supererogatory feature of laws, irrelevant to their inherent status – a facet not of what they are or need be, but the mere product of the epistemic uses to which they are put by reflective humans. Whatever the merits of this claim – and they are real – it is certainly not possible to take the same view of the 'nearer' sector of the realm of irreality, that of the unrealized dispositional and hypothetical variations of the real. It is crucial that any laws governing the melting point of lead apply to this leaden soldier and that it would have melted if it had been heated to $250°F$ (which is not the case). A thesis that does not govern the hypothetical variations of the real cannot qualify as a law. However incidental their application to fictive and 'merely possible' objects may be, the applicability of laws to the actualities of this world in a fact-altering manner is – albeit obtaining in merely the hypothetical domain – altogether crucial to the very lawfulness of purported laws.

Conceding hypothetical force as an ingredient in all *universal* laws of nature, one recent writer denies its applicability to law-fullness in general on the grounds that it is lacking in statistical laws.[10] Now to be sure when one develops the statistical law 'The half-life of californium is 5 hours' as basis for explaining why a particular atom of californium lasted $5\frac{1}{2}$ hours, then I cannot go on to say things like 'If this atom of uranium had been californium, then it would have lasted only $5\frac{1}{2}$ hours.' This sort of categorical and nonprobabilistic application of a statistical law is indeed impossible. But we surely can and would be prepared to say things like 'If this atom of uranium had been californium, then it would have had a halflife of 5 hours, and so the probability is .85 that it would have lasted only $5 \pm 1$ hours.' Statistical laws too can (and indeed *must*, if lawful) be capable of counter-factual applications – only in their case such applications will, naturally enough, take a probabilistic form.

That laws demand nomic necessity is one of the few points regarding which there is a substantial consensus in the history of philosophy. Aristotle insists on the matter in the *Posterior Analytics*.[11] It is a basic theme in Kant's *Critique of Pure Reason*.[12] And it continues operative in current writers. Such diverse authors as C. J. Ducasse, William Kneale, Ernest Nagel, and Arthur Pap, for example, hold that natural laws involve a necessity that is not logical but yet transcends merely *de facto* regularity.[13] Both Nelson Goodman and Roderick M. Chisholm

---

[10] Mario Bunge, *The Myth of Simplicity* (Engelwood Cliffs, N. J., 1963), p. 174.

[11] See especially sections 1–6 of Book I.

[12] See especially the Introduction and the Transcendental Analytic.

[13] See Curt J. Ducasse, 'Explanation, Mechanism, and Teleology,' *The Journal of Philosophy*, vol. 23 (1926), pp. 150–5; reprinted in H. Feigl and W. Sellars (ed's.), *Readings in Philosophical Analysis* (New York, 1949). William Kneale, *Probability and Induction* (Oxford, 1949), p. 258. Ernest Nagel, *The Structure of Science* (New York, 1961). Arthur Pap, *An Introduction to the Philosophy of Science* (New York, 1962),

have proposed hypothetical force as a prime criterion of the nomic necessity requisite for lawfulness.[14] And nowadays it is a matter of widespread agreement among philosophers that some characteristic mode of nomic necessity is involved in lawfulness, although there is much dispute as to just how the factor of nomic necessity is to be explicated. The writer of the pertinent article in the most recent philosophical encyclopedia puts the matter accurately by saying that the current point of dispute 'is not about the propriety of using such terms as "nomic necessity," rather it is about the interpretation of these terms or the justification of their use.'[15]

All the same, some recent writers have opted for a 'regularity theory' of laws according to which lawfulness is to be construed as unrestricted factual generality pure and simple, so that no implicit claim of nomic necessity is called for. The *locus classicus* of opposition to nomic necessity is J. S. Mill, who emphatically rejected any interpretation of laws as necessitarian.[16] But in fact, his own position, analyzing lawfulness in terms of *unconditionality* as well as mere *invariableness*, in effect yields the core of what nomic necessitarians demand.[17]

---

see chapter 16. Cf. also R. B. Braithwaite, *Scientific Explanation* (Cambridge, 1953), p. 293.

[14] R. M. Chisholm, 'The Contrary-to-Fact Conditionals,' *Mind*, vol. 55 (1946), pp. 289–307, reprinted in H. Feigl and W. Sellars (eds), *Readings in Philosophical Analysis* (New York, 1949). Nelson Goodman, 'The Problems of Counterfactual Conditionals,' *The Journal of Philosophy*, vol. 44 (1947), pp. 113–28, reprinted in L. Linsky (ed.), *Semantics and the Philosophy of Language* (Urbana, Ill., 1952), and in N. Goodman, *Fact, Fiction and Forecast* (Cambridge, Mass., 1955).

[15] R. S. Walters, 'Laws of Science and Lawlike Statements' in the *Encyclopedia of Philosophy*, ed. by P. Edwards, vol. IV (New York, 1967), pp. 410–14 (see pp. 411–12). This article offers a very clear and compact survey of the key issues regarding laws.

[16] *A System of Logic*, vol. II (London, 1843; 7th ed., 1868), pp. 419–21.

[17] For an interesting discussion of the historical issues see Gerd Buchdahl, 'Inductionist *versus* Deductionist Approaches in the Philosophy of Science as Illustrated by Some Controversies Between Whewell and Mill,' *The Monist*, vol. 55 (1971), pp. 343–67. For Mill see especially pp. 359–60.

A modern writer has attempted a somewhat similar line, contending that a leading

objection to the regularity theory is that it cannot account for possible instances. If this charge were indeed well founded, it would be difficult to see how one could avoid the view that natural laws assert some kind of necessity such that they apply in all possible worlds. However, it is not established that a defender of the regularity view cannot give a plausible account of the application of laws to possible instances. He would argue that statements about possible instances stand in the same kind of logical relation to a law as do statements about actual unobserved instances. To the extent that a law enables prediction about unobserved instances, it enables justifiable claims about unrealized possibilities.[18]

Now it is easy to see that this line of defense will not serve at all. It suffers from the critical defect of treating the unobserved and the unactualized cases in exactly the same way. But it is quite clear on even a little reflection that this step is indefensible, because the unobserved and the unreal are in a totally different position in the context of inductive considerations, since the realm of the (heretofore) unobserved lies open to observational exploration whereas the domain of the hypothetically unreal lies *ex hypothesi* beyond our reach. The very essence of inductive procedures is to warrant the step from observed to unobserved cases, whereas any law – whose very lawfulness arrogates to it nomological necessity and counterfactual force – takes not only this inductive step from observed to unobserved cases, but also takes the added step from actual to *hypothetical* cases, and specifically to cases which, being fact-contradicting, are in principle unobservable. The inductive justification of hypothetical force would have to take the form of a move from 'has always been applicable in counterfactual cases' to 'will always be applicable in counterfactual cases.' And the requisite premiss for such an

[18] R. S. Walters, *op. cit.*, pp. 413–14. At least one influential adherent of the regularity theory was, however, prepared to brush aside all references to the possible, saying 'Physics wants to establish regularities; it does not look for what is possible.' (L. Wittgenstein in his middle period as quoted by H. Speigelberg in the *American Philosophical Quarterly*, vol. 5 (1968), p. 256.)

F

induction must always obviously be unavailable. The unobserved and the unreal stand on an altogether different footing and must not to be conflated with one another.

Of course one could try to argue that the consideration of hypothetical cases is improper or illicit (illegitimate, 'beside the point,' or whatever), and that reality alone concerns us and that the unreal lies wholly outside the sphere of legitimate consideration. This does indeed abrogate the difficult nomic aspect of lawfulness. But it also writes off the prospect of hypothetical reasoning in the sciences and abolishes the concept of explanation as it has in fact developed in the setting of the Western tradition of scientific methodology.[19]

At this point, the following line of reasoning stands before us: (1) to accept a straightforward regularity view of natural laws is simply to give up the prospect of distinguishing between accidental and lawful empirical generalizations, and so to jettison the conception of natural law that has been operative in Western philosophy from the days of Plato and Aristotle to those of Nelson Goodman, Roderick Chisholm and Carl G. Hempel. And consequently, it is to abandon the concept of explanation in the West since antiquity, one that calls for the subsumption of the particular phenomena being explained under the covering generalizations of lawful purport. (2) But if the traditional conception of natural laws (as distinguished from simple regularities) is maintained, this requires us to recognize and acknowledge that central and defensive characteristic of laws: the fact that – through their essential support of counterfactual conditionals – they embrace applications to hypothetical as well as to actual cases and that existent and nonexistent states of affairs alike fall into their sphere of application. And just this relevance to the sphere of unrealized possibility renders laws reality-transcending in a way that essentially introduces their nomically

---

[19] This position is in fact taken by latter-day idealists of the type of F. H. Bradley and Brand Blanshard, who hold in effect that *nomic* necessity and *logical* necessity are actually indistinguishably one and the same, so that counterfactual hypotheses cannot be posed at all in any meaningful or coherent way. The serious drawbacks of such a view are relatively obvious.

necessitarian aspect. The crucial thing from the angle of present considerations is that if a law is *not* to be construed as having reality-transcending weight, then any prospect of its use in hypothetical reasoning is utterly destroyed.

## 2. LAWFULNESS AS MIND-INVOLVING

The pivotal conclusion of these considerations can now be elicited by way of a straightforward syllogism:

(1) Through their essential possession of nomic force, laws inevitably have a purview which embraces the sphere of that which is unactualized, and stake claims regarding not merely the actual, but the possible as well.

(2) The sphere of the possible is mind-invoking; in lacking reality a possibility does not exist in itself but only as an 'object of thought,' and as such its status is mind-relative.

(3) In invoking this mind-correlative domain, laws are consequently themselves mind-involving.

Laws deal quintessentially with the dispositions of actual things; and, of course, they can then – as we shall see – be projected beyond this realm to that of the merely possible as well. Though, of course, applicable to 'mere possibilities' as a matter of human *fiat*, laws deal – in the first and prime instance, at any rate – not with this remote sphere but with that of the potentialities of the real. And – as was argued at some length in the preceding chapter – this possibilistic domain is conceptually mind-involving in the analytical mode characteristic of the present discussion. There cannot be an *exhaustive* series of strictly objective, mind-independent facts corresponding to a law-thesis, because 'objective facts' must pertain to the real world of existing actuality, while the law has implications for and claims applicability to the sphere of unrealized possibility as well. The assertive content of a lawful thesis is possibility-referring, and thus fact-transcending, and therefore reality-transcending, and consequently mind-involving.

In saying that lawfulness involves a reference to the hypotheses and suppositions that render this concept mind-invoking we are not asserting simply – and trivially – that laws, being formulated in propositions, presuppose language, and therefore presuppose minds. It cannot be insisted upon too emphatically that it is *not* our concern to make the trivial point that to *state* or *express* or *assert* laws requires language and hence minds. This trivial truism is simply not at issue. The point is that the *content* of a law statement – i.e., the substantive claim made by asserting a general statement *as a law* – is something the logical dissection of which brings to view specifically mentalistic references, however tacit, to the hypothesizing capabilities of minds. Not merely the *conceptualizing* of a lawful world but *what is conceptualized* when that world is thought of *as lawful* is mind-involving. To say of a generalization that it is lawful and does not merely hold *de facto* is to paint it indelibly with the coloration of mind.

Lawfulness goes beyond the facts (not simply the *known* facts but the *existing* facts) because reality cannot be if-thenish. Nature must, of itself, be categorical: a state of affairs – any imaginable state – either exists or not, and that's that. And accordingly, any *type* of states of affairs is either always realized or sometimes or never. Given such types $P$ and $Q$, nature can be conjunctive (Sometimes: $P$-and-$Q$) or disjunctive (Always: $P$-or-$Q$). And it can be if-thenish in the essentially trivial mode of *material* implication (trivial, that is, *qua* mode of 'implication'):

$$P \supset Q \text{ for Never: } P\text{-and-}R \text{ (with } R = \text{not-}Q)$$

But nature cannot of itself – without transgressing the boundaries of the real – be if-thenish in any of the many stronger senses of 'implication' that are currently in philosophical vogue, among which the if-then implication of lawful connection must be located. For all of these require for their semantical explication some deployment of the conception of possible worlds other than the actual one.

At this juncture, however, the distinction between laws and regularities becomes critically important. No doubt nature is in various respects regular – it would take a bold act of rashness to deny that! And this regularity of nature in various respects is no doubt an ontological fact that would remain unaltered in the face of any hypothetical removal of rational minds from within its purview. But this is not the issue. The point, rather, is that the very idea of a law involves more than just factual regularity as such because lawfulness is bound up with nomic necessity and hypothetical force. To say that these factors do not represent purely objective facts, but make transfactual claims as well, is not to gainsay the objective reality of regularities in nature. Rather, it is to recognize that laws play a role in our conceptual scheme that imposes requirements going beyond mere regularity. A regularity will not just *be* a law, because laws will, and must in principle, behave differently from 'mere regularities' as such (e.g., in regard to inferential processes in the hypothetical mode). To regard a generalization as not just accidental but as endowed with the appropriate modal aspect of nomic force is already to view it as a genuine law. It is not the *regularity* claimed by a law but the *lawfulness* it builds into this claim that emerges from this analysis as mind-involving. (The 'idealist' aspect of our law-idealism is thus a qualified one.)

It must be stressed that we have no wish to deny the important distinction between the formulation of a fact and the fact as such, which would presumably continue quite unaltered if unformulated. What is denied, however, is that this fact-orientated distinction carries over to laws; a denial made precisely because laws proffer, on our analysis, a claim that is trans-*factual*. For it is maintained that the very substance of a law-thesis is in essential part inherent in its being maintained-as-a-law (and so conforming to a mind-relative condition). Accordingly its 'formulation' is essential to the lawfulness of a law in ways that the 'formulation' of a merely factual thesis is not essential to its factuality. Our theory thus claims for laws an assertive status that makes them in crucial respects mind-involving. To be sure, this mind-involvingness is of the conceptual sort basic to our discussion, and relates to the conceptual machinery operative in the formulation of law-theses, and not to their *content*. We are *not* saying (à la Hume) that all laws are in the final analysis laws of psychology. These considerations remove the objection that our analysis is such as to render untenable the surely plausible claim that there are laws no one will ever discover (or *assert* or *think of*). For what is mind-involving in laws, on our analysis, is not the regularity-claim that forms the crucial component of their content, but rather the actuality-transcending facets of lawfulness that are at issue with all genuine (hypothesis-supportive) law-claims.

The mind-involvement of lawfulness can be seen most vividly from a perspective already alluded to above. The thesis that 'Oak trees are (lawfully) deciduous' – that is, 'Oak trees *have to be* deciduous' in a sense that warrants 'If that pine were an Oak, then it would be deciduous' – does not deal with the 'objective fact' of regularity alone, but frames its claims about 'the facts' in such a way as to bring in a realm of the hypothetically possible which by the very nature of the hypothetical, is inherently mind-involving. Regularity calls for no more than a universal generalization of the type:

(1) All X is Y.

But lawfulness – as was insisted above – goes well beyond this to call for stipulations of the form:

(2) All X is Y, and if any $z$ that is not an X were an X, then $z$ would be a Y.

Now (1) is simply an issue of ontological fact: if it is in fact the case that *All (pure) mercury solidifies at −150° F*, then this circumstance could continue operative even if one abstracted from all reference to minds, overt and covert alike. But a type (2) generalization – a lawful generalization – would fare differently. Its reference to $z$'s which are not X's having to have certain characteristics if they were X's involves claims outside the domain of ontological fact, claims of which sense can be made only by the use of mind-invoking conceptions.

In a universe conceived on strictly amentalistic lines – one described without any reference, however tacit, to mentalistic conceptions – the whole domain of the hypothetical can find no foothold. Lawfulness in a very real sense 'lies in the eyes of the beholder,' since the lawfulness of a generalization consists in its being regarded and treated and classified and used in a certain way. All this is impossible in a 'mindless' world, i.e., a world described without any even oblique invocation of minds and their capabilities. Kant was quite right. Lawfulness is not something that one can meaningfully postulate in an objectively mind-independent manner – it is a mode of 'appearing to a mind.' For if the hypothetical element (which is clearly accessible only in a world endowed with minds) were *aufgehoben* (annihilated), lawfulness would be *aufgehoben* too. Of course, *we* can think of an 'alternative possible world' that is unpopulated, and so mindless, but yet lawful – so long as we do not ourselves abstain from deploying all mind invoking-concepts, so as to postulate a genuinely amentalistic universe in whose descriptive indication mind-involving conceptions have no place. But if we rigorously put aside *all* reference to the mental – overt and covert alike – then the hypothetically possible is lost, and lawfulness is lost with it. And just this is the ultimate foundation for our thesis that laws, involving as they do essentially hypothetical claims, are inherently mind-dependent. (To say all this is, of course, not to say that a world devoid of minds cannot be lawful. For our view construes the role of mind in a strictly conceptual rather than causal manner.[20])

Does this view of lawfulness entail the consequence that if there were no rational minds then there would be no natural laws? The answer is a *Yes* so heavily qualified as to amount to *No*. Given the concept of a law that we actually deploy for explanatory purposes, hypothetical force (and so nomic necessity) is an essential feature of a 'law.' The conception of lawfulness built into the very concept of a natural law involves an essential – if implicit – reference to the domain of supposition and counter-fact, to the hypothetical realm of 'what would happen if.' Since the sphere of hypothetical possibility is in the conceptual nature of things mind-involving, this will be the case also with respect to natural laws, which essentially involve reference to this domain through the contrast between laws and mere (potentially accidental) regularities. The fact remains crucial that the mind-involvement of laws is a *conceptual* dependence, not an *ontological* one.

[20] Thus the present articulation of an idealist position is not within the purview of Berkeley's dictum: ''tis wondrous to contemplate the world emptied of intelligences' (*Commonplace Book*, entry 23).

The conception of lawfulness maintained here places natural laws into a distinct and distinctive light. Laws claim more than mere regularity as such; for accidental universal truths also represent regularities, but cannot support counterfactuals in the manner quintessential to laws. But the laws at issue do not have the force and inviolability of *logical* truths: to gain the requisite necessary by *this* route is to pay too heavy a price. For we then could not (as in fact we can) reason coherently from contrary-to-law assumptions. ('If the law of gravitation were an inverse-cube relation instead of an inverse-square one, then . . .') On the present view, lawfulness is a halfway house between mere regularity and logical principle: its nomic necessity is stronger than mere *de facto* truth, but weaker than the logically apodeictic relations of abstract concepts. (Clearly, it is *natural* necessity that is at issue in a discussion of scientific laws: conceptual and logico-mathematical necessity does not fall within the purview of our analysis of transfactual claims regarding reality and is not shown mind-dependent by our arguments. One could well be a Platonic realist in mathematics and still accept the present idealistic mind-involving analysis of *natural* necessity.) Laws thus inhabit that area to which Hume would forbid all rational access: the domain between matters of fact on the one side and logical necessities on the other.

Of course, idealists of the old school (Bradley, Blanshard) would also not accept our conception of laws as a *via media* between mere regularities on the one hand and the logically necessary on the other. Indeed their reasoning seems to proceed by elimination: there is no such intermediary, and natural laws are not mere regularities, *ergo* they are truths of logic. Now, of course, one would incline to counter this position with the claim that there is nothing inherently self-contradictory about denying the laws of nature, while there is something self-contradictory about denying a logical truth. The old-line idealists will respond that law-denials will turn out to be self-contradictory once we have learned enough about the *system* of which they are a part. (It is certainly possible to hold a belief on grounds one believes to be empirical, but which later – in the light of a more sophisticated understanding of concepts – turns out to be logically necessary.) They hold that when science is complete – when 'all returns are in' and 'everything is said and done' – then all lawful relations will be revealed as somehow logically necessary. This (Blanshard's) position is akin to that of Leibniz: All empirical propositions are analytic although they will not appear so to our finite minds. This position is not patently untenable, but asks a great deal of our metaphysical credulity: it places a burden upon one's faith in ultimates that has little to recommend it.

\*     \*     \*

The key points of the argument developed in this discussion can now be summarized as follows:

(1) The concept of scientific explanation is such as to require *lawfulness* in the generalizations employed.

(2) Lawfulness requires the factors of nomic necessity and hypothetical force.

(3) Nomic necessity and hypothetical force both in significant measure go beyond the sphere of what can possibly be established by observation and experiment. We deal here with a domain whose basis is suppositional and thus altogether mind-correlative.

(4) Laws are accordingly in significant respects not discovered but made. To assert that a generalization is lawful, unlike a simple assertion of regularity, involves claims (viz., of nomic necessity and hypothetical force) that are mind-involving and cannot be rested simply upon objective matters of observed fact.

(5) Our position thus has the character of a qualified idealism. Lawfulness is not *just* a matter of the observable facts, but involves – through reference to the factors of nomic necessity and hypothetical force – an essential element of transfactual contention, and thus is in a crucial respect mind-involving.[21]

[21] Some of the ideas dealt with in this reasoning are discussed in a very illuminating way in A. C. Ewing, *Idealism: A Critical Survey* (London, 1934, 3rd ed., 1961); see chap viii, 'Idealistic Metaphysics.'

The sources of this conceptual mind-dependency must be analyzed in greater detail and the epistemic basis of claims-to-lawfulness clarified. This is the work of the next chapter.

### 3. CAUSALITY AS MIND-INVOLVING

It is well to be explicit about facing one rather immediate consequence of the doctrine of the mind-involvement of lawfulness: namely that *causality* will stand on exactly the same footing. To speak of causation is to invoke (however tacitly) the operation of causal laws. (That heating the water *caused* it to boil can only be maintained on a basis of some thesis of the general type of the causal law 'water boils when heated to 100° C – at sea-level altitudes.') That any discussion of causation in the scientific context is coordinate with an at least implicit reference to causal laws is a part of general agreement among present-day philosophers of science.[22] The very idea of a causal connection between events is deployed in a generalized way that envisages their relationship as governed by a law, a causal law. In this way, the argument inherent in our analysis of lawfulness as conceptually mind-dependent leads inexorably to an acceptance of the traditional idealistic view that causality is mind-dependent. Thus relative to our standard conceptual scheme, the mentalistic resource of counterfact is required, *via* lawfulness, for our conceptualized apprehension of the realm of causally interrelated fact. In somewhat Kantian terms, our experience of the real as a network of causality involves and presupposes a wider realm governed by the category of possibility. To consider a relationship among actual occurrences within the space-time framework in terms of a *causal* linkage, is to regard it in a setting of powers and potentialities that inevitably ramify into the fact-transcending and mind-involving sphere of 'what would happen if.'

[22] See Ernest Nagel, *op. cit.*, pp. 73–8. That causality is correlative with (a certain form of) lawfulness is a thesis that was already maintained by the Stoics in antiquity and that received its most emphatic modern re-emphasis in the philosophy of Kant, and becomes, after him, the common heritage of the whole range of philosophical 'schools,' positivists and empiricists included.

Causality will thus clearly manifest the possibility-referring aspect of lawfulness in general. Even as describing the height of an elm tree as 'larger than average' is to characterize it against the backdrop of a consideration of other *actual* elms, so describing its growth pattern causally, in lawful terms, is to characterize it against a backdrop of other possibilities, including unrealized ones. Descriptive qualifiers like 'average,' 'normal,' 'unusual,' etc. presuppose by way of implicit reference a background of other *actualities*; lawful and causal characterizations envisage by way of implicit reference a background of other (unactualized) *possibilities*. And such possibilistic involvements represent the locus of the conceptual mind-invocation implicit in the entire family of causality-related notions. Throughout, a possibilistic framework of reference is operative as essential background.

### 4. A SEEMING CIRCULARITY

The combination of our present argument that lawfulness is mind-invoking (because possibility-involving) with the previously argued contention that possibility is fundamentally law-involving (because it conceptually invokes reference to the *functioning* of minds) seems to move in a circle once we recognize the fact that lawfulness is inherent in any and all 'modes of functioning,' *mental* functioning very definitely included. In detail, this circle has the following structure:

(1) Possibility has been argued to be mind-involving because it conceptually involves reference to the *functioning* of minds (specifically their conceptualizing and hypothesizing functioning).

(2) The concept of function and modes of functioning obviously involves laws and lawfulness. (The very idea of function, process, or the like calls for lawfulness of operation.)

(3) Lawfulness has been argued to be mind-invoking because it implies possibility and possibility is mind-involving.

If this analysis of the pattern of our argumentation proves correct, then the reasoning is circular and, as it were, question-begging.

To break this circle it is necessary to draw an essential distinction, namely that between

(A) the *intellectual* functioning of minds in conceptualizing hypothesizing, identifying, reasoning, etc. (I-functioning) and

(B) the *causal* functioning of the processes and potentialities operative in the general run of things in nature (C-functioning)

The former is *explicitly* mind-referring; the latter is *conceptually* mind-involving (in ways to be argued below). Quite different sorts of mind-invocation are thus at issue in these two cases.

The circle in view can accordingly be broken by appealing to this distinction. Focussing on the pivotal terminus of item (3), we split this item into two components, as follows:

(3a) I-lawfulness is mind-dependent by its very nature, because explicitly *mental* functioning is at issue.

(3b) C-lawfulness is mind-invoking because it implies possibility, and

(i) Possibility is *conceptually* mind-involving because its analysis carries back, through hypotheticality, to the intellectual functioning of minds (I-functioning), but

(ii) I-functioning implies I-lawfulness, and *this* is mind-dependent for the reasons indicated on the opposite side of this tabulation (and so *not* for the reasons indicated at the head of *this* column).

We thus break the circle by drawing a due distinction between two orders of lawfulness and of functioning, the intellectual and the causal.

This approach brings to the fore one critical aspect of the matter of the mind-involvement of lawfulness: it suggests, and suggests rightly, that I-lawfulness (the lawfulness of minds and their capabilities and modes of functioning) is conceptually basic to lawfulness as a whole. It is this *paradigmatic* role of mind that marks our position as idealistic (rather than merely rationalistic).

Accordingly, our over-all position does not take the circular path outlined at the beginning of this section, but rather follows a linear route:

(1) The functioning of minds, or I-functioning as we have called it (in particular in respect to such processes as assuming, supposing, etc.), is the conceptual starting-point from which

(2) A conceptualistic theory of possibility is articulated, and then, in consequence we obtain

(3) A conceptualistic theory of laws in terms of which

(4) The generic functioning (C-functioning) of natural processes in general is conceptualized.

Thus minds and their processes are seen as the starting-point for the articulation of a conceptualistic theory of possibility (possibilities being seen as the product of mental construction), and this in turn provides the foundation for our conceptualistic theory of laws.

\*       \*       \*

Finally, the preceding considerations provide the materials for an answer to the objection inherent in the following question:

In the preceding chapters it was maintained that purely hypothetical possibilities are strongly (ontologically) mind-dependent and not just weakly (conceptually) mind-invoking, like less remote sorts of possibilities. But the present chapter has argued that genuine laws envisage applications to the whole range of possibilistic cases, specifically including the purely hypothetical ones. Would it not be necessary, in view of this, to strengthen the thesis of this chapter to hold that laws are *ontologically* mind-dependent, and not just *conceptually* mind-involving as was in fact maintained here?

The answer is negative. The commitment of lawfulness to merely hypothetical cases is hypothetical in form, not categorical. (It takes the form 'If a case – be it actual or hypothetical – conforms to certain conditions, then such-and-such principles will apply to it.') There is no outright commitment to hypothetical cases of an existentially assertive sort (i.e., nothing specific claimed as to any hypothetically extant thing or state of affairs). All that need occupy the stage of consideration is (1) the *intention* – insepar- able from a law-claim – to embrace actuality-transcending cases, and (2) the *disposition* of minds to the framing of hypotheses. Both of these factors (intentions and dispositions) lead us into the realm of mind-involving capabilities, in ways to whose detailed exploration a later chapter will be devoted. But the key fact for present purposes is that *this* sort of conceptual mind-invocation is as far as we need go in maintaining the mind-involvement of laws.

# Chapter V

# THE IMPUTATIONAL THEORY OF LAWS

## I. THE PROBLEM OF THE SOURCE OF NOMIC NECESSITY: THE INSUFFICIENCY OF EVIDENCE

The preceding chapter has argued at length that nomic necessity and hypothetical force are indispensable features of the laws used for the scientific explanation of events. This leads unavoidably to the question: Upon what evidential basis does an empirical generalization acquire the nomic necessity and hypothetical force it needs for lawfulness? It is clear upon reflection that however vast this evidential basis may be, and no matter how massively the substantiating data may be amassed through observation and experiment, and with whatever elaborateness the case may be developed, this evidential basis will always be grossly insufficient to the claim made when the generalization is classed as a law. This is so in part for the familiar reason that while all such evidence relates to the past and possibly the present, scientific laws invariably also underwrite claims about the future. Moreover, it is also made manifest when one considers the conceptual nature of lawfulness, bearing in mind that observation and evidence inevitably relate to what happens *in fact*, whereas laws invariably also underwrite claims of a hypothetical or counterfactual kind.

Consider this matter of the insufficiency of the evidential basis for a law somewhat more closely. It is obvious that this basis will be *deductively insufficient* – insufficient, that is, when the argument from the evidence to the law-thesis looked upon as being deductive – because the evidence inevitably relates to a limited group of cases while the applicability of the law is unrestricted.

Moreover, the evidential basis will also be *inductively insufficient*. For inductive procedures are designed to warrant the step from observed to unobserved cases, whereas a law – whose very lawfulness arrogates to it nomological necessity and counterfactual force – takes not only this inductive step from observed to *unobserved* cases, but also takes the added step from actual to *hypothetical* cases and specifically to cases which, being fact-contradicting, are in principle unobservable. The inductive justification of hypothetical force would have to take the form 'has always been applicable to counterfactual cases' to 'will always be applicable to counterfactual cases.' And the requisite premiss for such an induction must obviously always be evidentially unavailable. The evidential foundation for lawful generalization is thus afflicted with a twofold insufficiency, not only in the *deductive* mode, but also *inductively*, at any rate as long as induction is construed along anything like usual and standard lines.[1] For induction as we know it is in principle impotent to yield any support of the counterfactual component inherent in laws.

The fact is that the distinctive, transfactual content of a law is incapable *in principle* of receiving any *evidential* support along standard lines, because there can be no observational data regarding those instantiations (namely the counterfactual ones) that are distinctive of laws in contrast with the corresponding 'merely accidental generalizations.'

## 2. LAWFULNESS AS IMPUTATION

The basic point, a point whose importance cannot be overemphasized, is that the elements of nomic necessity and hypothetical force are not to be extracted from the evidence: they are not *discovered* on some basis of observed fact at all – they are *supplied*. It should almost go without saying that experience is of the actual alone: *the realm of hypothetical counterfact is inaccessible to observational or experimental exploration.*[2]

Lawfulness is thus not found in or extracted from the observational evidence, it is superadded to it.[3] *Lawfulness is the product*

[1] For a cogent attack on the view that laws can be established by induction see K. R. Popper, *The Logic of Scientific Discovery* (London, 1959), chap. III and New Appendix 10.

[2] It is obviously naïve to think that one can settle the question of the *counterfactual* application 'If Caesar's chariot had been a satellite in orbit about the earth it would have moved according to Kepler's laws' by increasing the domain of *actual* applications of Kepler's laws in putting more spacecraft into orbit.

[3] On this point our whole analysis is at one with Hume's position. Cf. *A Treatise of Human Nature*, Bk. III, Pt. I, section 14.

*of a transfactual imputation*: when an empirical generalization is designated as a law, this represents an epistemological status that is something which a generalization could not *in principle* acquire on the basis of warrant by the empirical facts. As Leibniz was wont to insist, the foundation for necessity must be sought in the mind, not in the senses:

. . . to return to *necessary* truths, it is generally true that we know them only by this natural light, and not at all by the experience of the senses. For the senses can very well make known, in some sort, what is, but they cannot make known what *ought to be* or what could not be otherwise.[4]

Men impute lawfulness to certain generalizations by according to them a particular role in the epistemological scheme of things, being prepared to use them in special ways in inferential contexts (particularly hypothetical contexts), and the like.

When one examines the explicit formulation of the overt *content* of a law, all one can ever find is a certain *generalization*. Their syntactic structure as universal propositions of conditional type is all that law statements have in common as statements. Its lawfulness is not a part of what the law *asserts* at all – it is no part of its formulation and is nowhere to be seen in its overtly expressed content as a generalization. Lawfulness is not determined by what the generalization *says*, but by *how it is to be used in our reasoning*. By being prepared to put it to certain kinds of uses in modal and hypothetical contexts, we, the users, accord to *a generalization its lawful status*, thus *endowing* it with nomological necessity and hypothetical force. Lawfulness is accordingly not a matter of the assertive content of a generalization, but of its epistemic status as determined by the ways in which it is deployed for explanatory and predictive applications and in hypothetical reasoning.

Consider, for example, the law 'Magnets attract iron filings' which supports the conditional 'If this iron bar were magnetized (which it isn't), then it would attract these iron filings.' As

---

[4] *The Philosophical Works of Leibniz*, ed. by G. M. Duncan (New Haven, 1890), p. 162. Compare also Kant's Second Analogy, especially at CPR, A196=B241, and cf. B3.

G

was argued in the preceding chapter, support of such counter-factuals is an indispensably essential feature of laws. Yet the establishment of such an inference drawn from fact-contravening hypotheses rests in the final analysis on a point of epistemological policy: the determination so to use 'genuine laws' (but *not* 'accidental generalizations') as to give them priority in the resolution of a contradiction-forced choice created by the introduction of contrary-to-fact hypotheses (in the manner illustrated above). This, however, is not a matter of what the law *states* but of what is to be *done* with it, and so its lawfulness does not inhere in the meaning-content of the law-statement, but derives from 'external' considerations, preeminently the precedence granted to it in counterfactual applications. Its being *lawful* is accordingly a feature of a generalization that is on much the same level with its being *axiomatic* or *important*: the issue is not one of the overt modes of formulation but of the uses to which it is put. (The axiomatic statement does not – and need not – *say* 'I'm an axiom' and indeed the one that does say so need not *be* so.) Lawfulness is not a matter of semantic content but of epistemic status. This formulation of the issue of course supposes the (scientifically standard) situation of laws formulated without the explicit use of the nomically modal *must*. But even if lawfulness were made thus explicit, the *point* of our discussion would remain unaffected.

By examining an isolated generalization we can no more settle the issue of whether it is 'really' a law than we can comparably settle the issue of whether an isolated mathematical thesis is 'really' an axiom. This axiomatic analogy holding that laws are essentially analogous to the axioms in a formalized system is crucial. It is notorious that there are many ways to axiomatize a given system, and that the decision to endow a certain family of propositions with axiomatic status is based on various extra-systematic considerations (ease and elegance in proof construction, efficiency in establishing metatheorems, convenience in opening the system to an interpretation, etc.). Similar considerations obtain regarding the decision to grant certain generalizations the status of laws. These considerations are largely pragmatic in nature, and have to do with the way the generalization in question fits into the fabric of our picture of the world. Clearly, on this approach, it is not the expressive *content* of a law that is mind-dependent – any more than the context of an axiom need be – rather, it is its *lawfulness* that is so dependent, just as with the axiomaticity of the axiom.

This approach to lawfulness as imputed rests on a conception of the nature of scientific laws to which more explicit articulation must be given. Present-day philosophers of science have concentrated their attention primarily upon two aspects of 'laws': (1) their *assertive characteristics,* having to do with the machinery deployed in their formulation (they must be universal generalizations, must be conditional in form, must make no explicit reference to time, must contain no overt spatial delimitation, they should be 'simpler' than equally eligible alternatives, etc.), and (2) their *evidential status,* having to do with the nature of their supporting data (they must have no *known* counterinstances, they should be supported by an ample body of confirming evidence, etc.).[5] To considerations of these two kinds one must, however, add a third quite different factor. This relates to the issue of *epistemic commitment* and is the extent to which we are committed to retention of the law in the face of putative discordant considerations of a strictly hypothetical character (and thus not of an *evidential* sort, for this would lead back to item (2) above). The appropriateness of such epistemic commitment revolves about questions of the type: 'To what extent is the "law" at issue justifiably regarded as immune to rejection in the face of hypothetical considerations?' 'How should this generalization fare if (*per improbabile*) a choice were forced upon us between it and other laws we also accept?' 'How critical is it that the law be true – how serious a matter would it be were a law to prove false?' To claim a generalization as a law is not to assert that it is in principle unfalsifiable; but it does maintain that its actual falsification would have very serious wider repercussions for the fabric of our knowledge.

[5] See, for example, the excellent discussion in chap. 4 of Ernest Nagel's book on *The Structure of Science* (New York, 1961).

### 3. THE WARRANT FOR IMPUTATION

While it is, of course, 'we' who 'decide' upon the placement of a law in the epistemological scheme of things, and 'we' who make an 'epistemic commitment' to the law, the crucial point is that this be done on the basis of rational grounds (of complex and varied character), and not on the basis of a merely random choice or personal predilection. The appropriateness of epistemic commitment to laws is therefore *not* a matter of psychology or of the sociology of scientific knowledge. For one thing, it is necessary and proper to distinguish between being *in fact* committed to accepting a generalization as a 'law' of more or less fundamental status upon the one hand, and being *properly* or *warrantedly* committed to it, upon the other. To be sure, lawfulness can never be derived wholly from an observational foundation. But it represents an imputation that is (or should be) well-founded upon evidential grounds. The key factors in this well-foundedness are the *correspondence-to-fact* aspect of empirical evidence and the *systematic-coherence* aspect of fitting the generalization into a fabric of others that in the aggregate constitute a rational structure, an integrated body of knowledge that constitutes a 'branch of science.'

While laws are indeed man-made, they are not thereby made as man *wants* them. In maintaining that the necessity and hypotheticality of lawfulness are matters of imputation, we thus have no wish to suggest that the issue is one of indifferent conventions or arbitrary decisions. The imputation is, to be sure, an overt step for which a decision is required. But to be *justified* this decision must be based upon a rational warrant, and must have its grounding in (1) the *empirical evidence* for the generalization at issue in the law, and (2) the *theoretical context* of the generalization. Such evidential and systematic grounding is required to provide the necessary *warrant* to justify an imputation of lawfulness. Since an element of imputation is involved, laws are not just discovered, they are, strictly speaking, made. But this is not, of course, to say they are made arbitrarily. Although they cannot be extracted from the empirical evidence, they must never contravene it. Such conformity with 'the observed facts' is a key factor of that complex that bears the rubric of *well-foundedness*.

Our conception of the origin of the key requisites for a law (nomic necessity and fact-transcending hypotheticality) can thus be summarized in the slogan: *Lawfulness is the product of the well-founded imputation to empirical generalizations of nomic necessity and hypothetical force.* Both of these two factors, the essentially factual element of well-foundedness and the essentially decisional element of imputation, are necessary to laws. Well-founding is essential because the very spirit of the scientific enterprise demands reliance only upon *tested* generalizations that have a solid observational or experimental basis. But the element of imputation is also essential, since – as emphasized above – we can only observe what *is*, i.e., forms parts of the realm of the actual, and not what corresponds to the modally necessary or the hypothetically possible. The nomic necessity and hypothetical force characteristic of lawfulness thus represent factors that a generalization cannot conceivably earn for itself on the basis of observational or experimental evidence alone: it has to be *endowed* with these factors. The basic aspect of a lawful proposition is on this view not the *qualitative* aspect of being-a-law but the *relational* aspect of being-maintained-as-a-law. Lawfulness is in the final analysis a relational rather than an absolute and purely descriptive feature.

We must pursue somewhat further this key theme of the warrant for imputations of lawfulness, which we have held to be a question of evidence and of systematic context. The topic of *evidence* for generalizations may at this time of day be supposed to be relatively familiar to the reader. Even elementary discussions of scientific method devote considerable attention to the analysis of the evidence needed for scientific laws: the nature of evidential considerations, the evaluation of weight of evidence, and the like. On the other hand, the bearing of the systematic context of an empirical generalization in establishing its claims to lawfulness is a perhaps much less familiar issue.

It is not for nothing that branches of science are called *bodies* of knowledge. Scientific knowledge has a complex and highly articulated *structure*. The laws comprising this structure rarely if ever stand isolated and alone: they are part of a fabric whose threads run off to intertwine with other laws. Scientific laws do not stand in splendid isolation, they interlink with others in the complex logical structures commonly called *theories*. To say this is not to deny that there can be such things as 'merely empirical generalizations' – universal propositions which, though well-confirmed by the empirical evidence, wholly lack a footing within some ramified theoretical framework. Historically, Kepler's laws of planetary motion, Galileo's law of falling bodies, and Boyle's gas law, for example, were all well-established and generally accepted prior to securing the grounding provided by a foundation upon some theory. But an aggregation of well-confirmed empirical generalizations does not constitute a science. A science is not a catalogue of observed regularities. It requires a certain *rational architectonic*, relating a variety of empirical generalizations in a rational structure that exhibits their conceptual relevance and their explanatory interconnections. A well-established generalization qualifies as a *scientific law* (in the proper sense of the term) only when it finds its theoretical home within some scientific discipline or branch of science. (And, of course, the generalization does not change its *meaning* when it finds such a home, a fact that again bears out our point that lawfulness is a matter of external status rather than internal meaning-content.) As long as a generalization stands isolated as a relationless datum for which no theoretical rationalization is to be had in terms of the environing facts of science, its scientific status is at best tentative and problematic: it provides questions rather than answers and does not qualify for the dignity of a 'law of nature'. (Think of the status of Kepler's '*laws*' of before and after the work of Newton.)

This systematic factor represents an aspect of laws *crucially important to their status as laws*. For no matter what the structure of a generalization might be, or how well established it is by the known data, its acceptance *as a law* demands some accommodation of it within the 'system' of knowledge. Any 'law' occupies a place that is more or less fundamental within the general architectonic of our knowledge about the world – its epistemic status is a matter not only of *its own* form and *its own* evidential support, but of *its placement within the woof and warp of the fabric comprising it together with other putative laws of nature*. The standing accorded to it within the overall framework of our knowledge reflects our 'epistemic commitment' to the law, which is thus a matter not of the individual characteristics of the law viewed (insofar as possible) in isolation, but of its interconnections with and its epistemic rooting among other laws to which we are also committed. We must *decide* upon the epistemic status or ranking of the law with respect to others, and this decision, while in part guided by evidential factors, is not totally determined by them alone. It is a matter of a wide range of systematic considerations, among which evidential issues are only one (thought to be sure a prominent) factor. Lawfulness is accordingly a matter neither of *content* nor of *evidential basis* but of systematic status in an epistemic setting.

Yet, as we have seen, the conditions that establish a generalization as *law-like* – that is, as rationally *qualified* for an imputation of lawfulness on the basis of the usual methodological considerations – do not suffice to *establish* it as a law, i.e., as actually *lawful*. They fail in this because acceptance of a claim to lawfulness extends well beyond the factual basis upon which it is justified. To class a generalization as *law-like* is to say it is a *candidate-law* on the basis of factual consideration, but to class it as *lawful* is to step beyond this claim into the realm of nomic necessity and hypothetical force.

In saying that laws are man-made – that they are the products of a human decision to accord a certain status to specific generalizations – we do not intend to turn our back upon the work of methodologists of scientific inquiry and theorists of inductive logic. Insofar as their findings conform to the actualities of scientific practice there is no reason why we cannot – or should not want to – accept them in full. We are certainly not attempting a Quixotic substitution of 'free decision' for scientific method. But we regard the principles of the theory of scientific method from our own perspective and view them in what may well be a nonstandard light. From our standpoint they are *not* procedures for the *establishment* of generalizations as lawful; rather, they are procedures for providing the rational warrant for imputations of lawfulness.[6] The credentials of scientific method as the procedure for providing such rational warrant – both pragmatic (in terms of their practical fruitfulness) and Darwinian (in terms of the processes of historical selection on the basis of proven successes) – are altogether impressive and, in effect, decisive. It cannot be said too emphatically that the theory of lawfulness as imputation does not come to destroy the accepted procedures of scientific inquiry but to fulfill the claims to law-validation generally made on their behalf. Our approach does not deny but insists upon the crucial role of orthodox scientific method.

### 4. THE PURPORTED ANTHROPOMORPHISM OF LAWFULNESS

The general structure of this view of lawfulness as man-made is by no means novel. Various writers have long argued that the very idea of lawfulness is at bottom anthropomorphic.[7] The basic concept is that lawful phenomena are *rule-governed*: the conception of operative rules lies at the conceptual foundation of lawfulness. But this idea – it is argued – ultimately originates in man's first hand experience of the rules of his social group:

[6] The first methodologist of science to take a position something like this was W. Whewell, who argued that (1) genuine laws must have the modal aspect of universality and necessity, (2) this can never be arrived at by reasoning from experience, and so requires a *sui generis* process ($\cong$ our *imputation*), which 'is not reasoning: it is another way of getting at truth,' but (3) the offering of justified law claims must have a proper empirical basis ($\cong$ Whewell's 'consilience of inductions'). The objections of modern critics to this procedure (see Laurens Laudan, 'William Whewell on the Consilience of Inductions,' *The Monist*, vol. 55 [1971], pp. 368–91; see especially pp. 282–3) may be met by noting that Whewell does not offer the (self-contradictory) claim that the empirical basis establishes lawfulness in a *demonstrative* mode, but only that it warrants a rational claim to lawfulness in a *presumptive* mode. Whewell may not overtly have espoused the imputational theory of lawfulness, but once one does so, all of his characteristic doctrines on the subject would fall smoothly into place.

[7] For an illuminating discussion of historical issues see Edgar Zilsel, 'The Genesis of the Concept of Physical Law,' *The Philosophical Review*, vol. 51 (1942), pp. 3–14.

rules of behavior, of speech, of worship, of dress, etc. The 'pressure' of social rules and their associated sanctions is something of which each man is conscious in his own mind. On this theory, the rule-conformity of this social context is projected into external nature to provide the concept of natural lawfulness, analogizing the regularity of natural phenomena to those of the social realm In thus viewing man's first-hand experience of social rules as the foundation for his projection of nomic force into the laws of nature, one sees the subjective tendency of mind as the model for lawfulness and the ultimate source for the imputation of nomic necessity that is the touch-stone of laws. From this perspective mind itself appears as the basic model of lawfulness and causality. Its own urge for system, organization and stability through rules, regulations, and patterns that facilitate our dealings throughout the sphere of human affairs is held to provide the mind with a conceptual basis for the imputation of universality and necessity in the processes of nature.

Other writers see mind as paradigmatic for causality because of our first-hand experience of the control we exercise over our own processes of thought and over the actions of our bodies. On this approach, the will (= person-causality) is the paradigm of natural causality in general. We reach the conception that in the exercise of our own wills we ourselves provide the basis of experiential contact with causal efficacy sought by thinkers of a Humean stamp. This position was, in effect, prefigured in Leibniz, and it is implicit in Kant and clearly explicit in Schopenhauer.

Such a theory of the anthropomorphic genesis of the concept of lawfulness finds its natural companion in a cognate view of the genesis of the conception of possibility, a view which sees the foundation of the conception in the sphere of intentional action, specifically in the control over our own bodies whose acquisition in infancy is a basic aspect of human development. Intentional action, of course, cries out for a dispositional analysis ('If my hand is moved in this way, then I bring the spoonful of porridge to my mouth'). Accordingly, it is held that our recognition of the control we have of our bodies and their components, and our awareness of the dispositional aspect of our capabilities ('If I do . . ., then I bring . . . about') is the soil in which there grows our concept of possibility in general and so of specifically unactualized possibilities. (From this standpoint it is only natural that the protoexplanation of natural phenomena should be given in animistic terms.) On such a view the basic model for our concept of the 'natural possibility' inherent in the powers and characteristic modes of functioning of things in nature is seen to lie in a fundamentally anthorpomorphic source. The human will becomes the paradigm for the development of the conceptions of power, potentiality, and process as we deploy them throughout our conception of nature.[8]

Be it as it may with all such conjectures as to the specific manner of the psychological genesis of the ideas of hypothetical possibility and nomic necessity, there remains the key fact of the *conceptually* mind-involving nature of these ideas. And this suffices to indicate the mind-involving ramifications of that conception of lawfulness for which they serve as indispensable constituents.

### 5.  THE HERITAGE OF HUME AND KANT

This view of the nature of lawfulness carries Kant's Copernican revolution one step further. Hume maintained that faithfulness to the realities of human experience requires us to admit that we cannot find nomic necessity in nature. Kant replied that such necessity does indeed not reside in observed nature, but rather in the mind of man, which projects lawfulness into nature in consequence of features indigenous to the workings of the human intellect.[9] Both Kant's and Hume's views share the

[8] For the thesis that human agency is the historically primary causation see, e.g., R. G. Collingwood, *An Essay on Metaphysics* (Oxford, 1940), pp. 285ff.

[9] A thread running through much of the history of philosophy is the thesis that there would be no laws if there were no lawgiver; that the universe would not be intelligible by man if it were not the product of a creative intelligence. We find this theme in Plato's *Timaeus*, in the cosmological argument of St Thomas Aquinas and the schoolmen, in Descartes and Leibniz, in Butler's *Analogy* and the tradition of natural theology in England. Leibniz puts the matter cogently and succinctly: '. . . the final analysis of the laws of nature leads us to the most sublime principles of order and perfection, which indicate that the universe is

characteristic aspect of our own position in having the consequence that laws, even natural laws, are in some measure *made*
by man rather than being altogether products of his *discovery*.

Our view of the matter agrees with Hume that lawfulness is not
an observable characteristic of nature, and it agrees with Kant
that it is a matter of man's projection. But we do not join Kant
in seeing this projection as the result of the (in suitable circumstances) *inevitable* working of the psychological faculty-structure
of the human mind. Rather, we regard it as a matter of *warranted
decision*, a deliberate man-made imputation effected in the setting of a particular conceptual scheme regarding the nature of
explanatory understanding. We thus arrive at a position that is
Kantian with a difference. Kant finds the source of lawfulness in
the way in which the mind inherently works. We find its source in
the conceptual schemata that we in fact deploy in the rational
structuring of our experience, above all in context of our explanatory purposes. As we see it, lawfulness demands an imputational
step made in the context of a certain concept of explanation.

## 6. DOES THE SUCCESS OF SCIENCE INVALIDATE THIS POSITION?

The following deceptively straightforward objection may well be
offered to the view that lawfulness is imputed:

> The high degree of internal order present in, say, a DNA
> molecule is wholly independent of the acts of minds. It is pre-
> cisely calculable in terms of information bits and certainly
> exists objectively, wholly apart from any ascriptions or impu-
> tations we humans might make.

And, of course, there is a great deal of truth in this objection. No
one wants to deny the common sense precept that 'the real facts'

---

the effect of a universal intelligent power.' (G. W. Leibniz, *Philosophical
Papers and Letters*, ed. by L. E. Loemker, vol. II [Chicago, 1956], pp.
777–8.) In this tradition, Kant's 'Copernican Revolution' is decisive.
Kant in effect agrees with the underlying thesis that the intelligibility
and rationality of the universe must be the work of an intelligent and
rational mind, but shifts the application of the principle from the
*creator* of the natural universe to the *observer* of it.

are what they are, independently of our human doings. But lawfulness is, as we have insisted, *transfactual*, and this critical aspect calls for that element of human 'decision' which we have characterized as an imputation. Yet obviously, in taking this imputational step we are not free, but remain subject to the massive restraints of the course of natural events.

The massive and striking success of the sciences in enabling us to predict and control the course of natural events may seem at first sight to militate against the acceptability of our position. If the fabric of natural laws and the causal order of the universe are seen as being in significant measure *the product of a mental construction*, how are we to square this with their dramatic success in scientific prediction and control?

From our approach this *seeming* difficulty is not a real one. To be sure, natural laws according to our theory possess a substantial element of imputation and postulational construction. But as has been stressed again and again, this is not a matter of *free* construction and *arbitrary* imputation. Our insistence on the element of well-foundedness and our adoption of the standard canons of scientific method for this purpose provide the means of mitigating the mentalistic factor of imputation. And, in particular, the thesis that laws are linked to objective regularities in nature holds our feet to the ground in considering the 'constructive' aspect of laws. (We have, to be sure, insisted that regularities *underdetermine* laws. A regularity – any perfectly genuine regularity – could be conceptualized as merely accidental, simply by not adding that 'something more,' the mind-involving factors of nomic necessity and hypothetical force indispensable for a claim of lawfulness.)

The idea – inherent in our position – that 'the causal order of the world is a mental construct' may at the very first seem absurd and repellent.[10] And deservedly so if there were no compensatory

---

[10] Perhaps not so much so from a contemporary perspective. For note that the mind-involvement of causation is a trivial consequence of any view that holds that cause/effect relations 'are intelligible only against a pattern of theory.' (N. R. Hanson, *Patterns of Discovery* [Cambridge, 1958], p. 64.) And this view is close to orthodoxy among contemporary philosophers of science.

stress that this construction is not free or arbitrary but must be well-founded and circumscribed by due heed of the established canons of scientific practice. Subject to such qualifications, however, it seems to me that the strangeness and unpalatability of the position evaporates. The success of science is no more inexplicable on our 'idealistic' position than on any 'realistic' rival. Indeed, the case is very much one of parity on both sides. Where the one approach speaks of the 'discovery of a law' (and immediately runs into the Humean difficulties of the justification of induction), the other speaks of 'the warranting of an imputation of lawfulness' (and avoids these particular difficulties at one bold stroke). But given this difference of perspective all else is – with but minor readjustments – left pretty much the same. Both approaches demand the bridging of an evidential gap, a transition the 'realistic' theory sees as available in Hume-rebutting terms, and the 'idealistic' theory in concept-scheme-justifying terms. The 'realistic' approach collides with the fact that our evidence-in-hand can never come close to establishing the full spectrum of claims built into a law thesis. Our 'idealistic' approach regards the conceptual scheme we employ as so operative that no transfactual justification is called for, since all that is needful is built into the workings of the imputation-laden concepts themselves. (This leaves the problem that such an imputation-laden scheme not be justified in some way, but this turns out to be a very different and emphatically *pragmatic* story.) An explanation of the success of science is called for on both sides of the divide, and turns out to be no more problematic on the idealistic than on the realistic approach. On the contrary, theoretical justification along the idealist/pragmatic lines is to all appearances more straightforward and satisfactory.[11]

## 7. IMPUTATIONS RECONSIDERED

It is useful to supplement the preceding treatment of the imputational theory of laws with some remarks about imputation or postulation as a methodological device of wider applicability.

[11] Some of the materials for the preceding parts of this chapter are taken from the writer's book *Scientific Explanation* (New York, 1970).

Indeed, the procedure of imputation is particularly important from the standpoint of a wide spectrum of rationalist points of view, owing to the inherent plausibility of the thesis that 'the constitutive contribution of the mind to our knowledge of the world' is made by way of imputations (as implicit in a conceptual scheme).

This is particularly clear whenever a reality-characterizing claim goes beyond the confines of all possible experience and observation, that is, whenever a leap beyond the possibly available evidence is made under the aegis of a conceptual scheme – exactly as we saw to be the case with respect to laws. The constructive contribution of mind is particularly notable whenever our claims regarding reality attribute to it features that could not possibly be warranted as a matter of 'observationally given fact.'

The 'problem of other minds' affords a paradigm example. All that one can ever 'observe,' in any relatively strict sense, is someone's behavior (e.g., his grimacing) but we conceptualize this mentalistically and so do not hesitate to say, quite properly, that we *see that* he is in pain (without in any way doing that impossible thing of seeing or sensing his pain). When we see his pain behavior we simply assimilate this case to our own situation 'in similar circumstances' (e.g., when cut and bleeding). Knowing in first-hand experience that such occurrences are painful (to us) we project this by way of imputation to others. This imputational aspect marks the fact that the 'seeing' of 'seeing *that* he's in pain' is done not merely with the eye of the body but with the mind's eye.

From this perspective, the crucial facts are these: (1) There is a decisive barrier between the manifestation of pain behavior on the one hand and the affective feeling of pain on the other – their fusion 'in our own case' notwithstanding. (2) This barrier is not to be crossed by any valid sort of *inference* from behavioral premises to an affective conclusion. Rather, (3) it is leapt by an imputation that is built into a conceptual scheme determinative of the ground-rules governing our application of pain-talk.

This example and that of laws is, as we see it, typical of that vast range of cases where the evidence-in-hand is in principle inadequate to the conclusion claimed. Thus, the leap from appearance ('$X$ appears on the basis of observational inspection to have feature $F$') to reality ('$X$ in fact has the feature $F$'), or again from teleological behavior of a sufficiently sophisticated kind to the possession of intelligence ('Can machines think?') are also essentially analogous to that of the leap from *post hoc* correlation to *propter hoc* causal connection that so troubled Hume and his latter-day congeners.

In all of these cases a decisive categorial barrier lies in the path of the direction of reasoning

> systematically observed instances ———→ laws
> pain behavior ———→ feelings of pain
> correlation ———→ causation
> appearance ('seems') ———→ reality ('is')
> teological behavior ———→ intelligent behavior

In such cases we cannot get from the left-hand item to the right-hand one by any sort of sound inference based on the observations in hand because we cannot secure the major premiss to warrant such an inference. In all cases we accomplish the rational transition at issue not by way of inference but by way of a mind-contributed imputation. But such an imputation is not a matter of human psychology (this is where Hume erred), but rather, it is built into the rational deployment of a conceptual scheme, and so has nothing personally idiosyncratic about it.

Thus, on such an approach, it is the logical placement of an imputation (postulation, rationally based assumption) within the framework of a conceptual scheme that is the crucial consideration. The imputation takes us beyond 'the actual evidence in hand' but the entry of the conceptual scheme means that this is done in a rational, duly warranted, and objective, or at any rate impersonal and interpersonal manner.[12]

This imputationism, however, carries us no further than rationalism: the doctrine that the mind makes a crucial constitutive contribution to the content of nature-as-we-conceive-it. As a general doctrine it does not go as far as idealism because

[12] Some further discussion of issues relating to this imputationism is given in sect. 3 of chap. X below.

the imputation in view, though of course made by a mind, need not be made in mentalese terms with a reliance upon models and paradigms that relate to minds and their functioning.

On the present view, the mind-invokingness of lawfulness accordingly does not reside in the imputational theory as such, but derives from our position that the imputation is made in terms of reference to the domain of possibility and that this the specific sphere of the possible, is mind-invoking for reasons set out in Chapters II and III. This imputational perspective helps to clarify one important aspect of our theory: its stress upon *conceptual* mind-involvingness. For on this imputational approach, the relationship to mind is located in the internal meaning-structure of the concepts that we use, to be duly revealed by an *analysis* of their implicit commitments, and so differs from the ontological mind-dependency of what pertains by way of explicit reference to minds and their workings.

But the question remains: What justifies an imputation? In general, an imputation represents a constitutive thesis adopted on regulative grounds, as part of the venture of the theoretical rationalization of our experience. In the final analysis its status is methodological and its justification is accordingly to be given in the pragmatic terms of 'working out' – of proving itself a successful instrument for the realization of the tasks in hand. And, of course, in the special case of imputation of lawfulness, the rational warrant is given in the first instance through an invocation of the canons of scientific method and in the final instance through more elaborately pragmatic considerations. But this line of justificatory argumentation involves large and far-reaching issues that cannot be treated here.[13] The crucial fact is that the imputational approach is not dogmatic but, admitting the need for rational support, seeks to develop it on an ultimately pragmatic basis.

[13] For an extensive treatment of the writer's views on these issues see his book *Scientific Explanation* (New York, 1970).

# Chapter VI

# PARTICULARITY AS MIND-INVOLVING

## 1. INTRODUCTION

We arrive at one of the key theses of our argument and one of the most controversial. For it will now be maintained that particularity is mind-invoking.

A *particular* – and let us now think of actual rather than merely possible particulars – a particular is a definite bit of concrete reality that has a distinct individuality of its own; it stands alone with its own unique individuality, a discrete item, a thing separate and distinct from all the rest of nature. Now just exactly what is the force of the phrase 'separate and distinct' here? Clearly the issue here is not merely one of *spatial* separateness, but rather has to do with its being an item distinct from all others in ways that perhaps *may*, but certainly *need not necessarily* involve spatial separation or exclusion. This leads at once to the key issue of the identification of particulars, since its distinct identity is an indispensably necessary feature of a particular as the very thing it is. As the Scholastic precept *ens et unum convertuntur* suggests, the very being of a particular lies in its susceptibility to identification, to its possession of a distinguishing individuality. But the very idea of an individual calls for the existence of criteria of identity to specify how it would be identified and discriminated from other individuals, etc. And a 'criterion' is an inherently mind-invoking conceptual resource. Accordingly, particularity is mind-involving in the conceptualistic manner of our theory.

## 2. THE PROBLEM OF IDENTIFICATION

To identify something is to characterize it descriptively or to indicate it ostensively or somehow else distinguish it from other things. But it is surely an unproblematic and indeed even a superficial point that all the modes of identification are mind-involving interactions. A basically interpersonal *transaction* is

H

always at issue here – describing, discriminating, pointing out, distinguishing, and so forth, invariably have a person as indirect object: they are transactions involving what someone, some agent, does for another (or for himself – in the special case).[1] Such interpersonal interactions in which one person so acts as to indicate something to a comprehending interlocutor have the common feature that *the attention of a mind is so directed as to be brought to focus upon something.* Identification is, by its very nature, a mentalistic *act*: 'to identify' is an intellectual process and 'to be identified' is accordingly a mind-invoking condition. The very concept of identification involves some reference to the directable attention of a comprehending intelligence.

Thought or discourse cannot coherently deal with a particular as 'a thing as it is in itself' but *must* consider things under such-and-such a description. Objects must be *thought of* – exactly as they must be *seen* – from a perspective or 'point of view.' (Of course, with thought, unlike seeing, it is an *intellectual* perspective and not an optical one that is at issue: the perspective of a certain family of concepts.) Now it is a virtually trite point that the *description* of any real thing or state of affairs is conceptually perspectival, and it is not hard to see that this must also go for its (criterion-relative) *identification.* In consequence, the conception we have of any particular empirical thing or state of things is an aspectival construct devised in an essentially mind-involving way.[2]

The objects about which we think and talk are generally *introduced* into the arena of thought and discussion not bodily and in themselves, but through their conceptual representatives. Our framework of concepts, and the conceptual points of view

---

[1] Thus spots in the visual field, identifiable to no one save the subject himself, qualify as identifiable items. The identificatory transaction is multi-personal in the *standard* cases, but not always; paradigmatically and generally, but not inevitably.

[2] Moreover, if the things of our standard conceptual scheme are only to be identified (individuated) through the use of predicates, if these predicates are inherently manifest (= observational) in character and if it can be shown that such manifest predicates are mind-invoking then we have a cogent argument to establish the mind-dependency of thinghood. For a tracing out of this line of thought, see Chapter VIII.

they make possible, play a key role in shaping 'our world.' Mind is the organizer of 'things,' and the *inevitable* presence of a mind-contributed perspective in any conception of natural particulars is a critical factor in constituting 'our world,' i.e., the-world-as-we-conceive-of-it. Of course, when particulars are at issue that actually happen to be present upon the stage, being physically at hand, they may be indicated ostensively (i.e., pointed out). Then our task of ferreting out mind-dependency is even simpler: ostension is by nature an attention-directing device. Moreover, ostension will invariably have a representative aspect: the element of 'representation' enters through the use of sortal qualifications inevitable even in ostensive identifications, e.g., 'that *cat* (pointing).'

The mechanisms for introducing particulars into the setting of thought and discussion bring them into this light under a certain *perspective of consideration*. Just as physical objects cannot be *seen* free from the limitations of a *physical* 'point of view,' so things cannot be considered or discussed free from the limitations of a *conceptual* 'point of view.' Just as things must be seen under aspects, so they must be conceived or considered under aspects: 'under a certain description,' as current jargon has it. One can separate the particular itself from any one particular single description or mode of reference to it, but if this thing is going to be considered or discussed at all, this must, of course, be done from *some* conceptual perspective or other. It is at this point, as I shall argue, that the factor of mind-dependency most markedly enters in. The object is not introduced as such, but relative to a specified mode of identifying characterization. When that characterization is itself mind-involving, then so is the complex that is the object-under-that-characterization.

Identification requires minds: even as the camera arrests a process in midcourse to yield the picture of a static situation nowhere to be encountered in nature itself, so mind in identifying deploys criteria of identity of its own devising in carving reality up into discrete units. In regard to particularity, the process-philosophers were on the right track. From our perspective, the picture painted by James and Bergson of the active role of mind in carving discrete things from a continuous flux is helpful. Think of James' picture of the mind as imposing the arresting impetus of conceptual structure upon the blooming, buzzing confusion of natural flux. Without the focusing power of concepts, the mind is like a camera badly out of focus that permits no discrimination of specific individuals. Such an analogy suggests – quite correctly – the mental construction of the particulars of our world, and so indicates the inherent mind-dependence of particularity.[3] (On the other hand, any such representational analogy is seriously defective in its implicit suggestion that the specific individuals 'are there' all right, but only *presented* confusingly.)

We regard the things of the world in terms of an intellectual framework of concepts: we not only think of things but even see them (literally *see* them) in framework-conditional terms. The conceptual mechanisms of our language accordingly play a critical role in the determination of the feature of our world.

Our position bears some analogy with Kant's. For him, particular-individuation is only possible subject to a *framework of categories* that *necessarily* characterize the domain of the *possible experience* of things. For us, particular-individuation is only possible subject to a *framework of concepts* that *in fact* characterizes the domain of the *possible discrimination* (distinguishing) of things. In either case, the conception of particularity stands in an essential relationship to a mentalistic function (experiencing, distinguishing) in such a way as to render it indispensably mind-referring. Our position, like Kant's, relies heavily on the central role of mind-contributed criteria of identity and individuality as crucial to the conception of a particular thing.

### 3.  IDENTIFIABILITY VS. IDENTIFICATION

But the impact of the argument that identification is mind-involving is tempered by the following line of objection: 'Let it be granted (says the objector) that your argument has shown

---

[3] Leibniz is quite right in his view that 'ultimate' reals must lie outside the domain of possible experience. Our position carries back to his thesis that the unity of the things of our empirical experience is mind-supplied and lies as it were 'in the eyes of the beholder'; but it is mediated through Kant's teaching that the unity of empirical objects is *thematic* in character, and as such represents an interpretative factor that implements certain mind-imposed *requisites* for thinghood (CPR, B114).

that to say '*X* is *identified*' is to make a mind-referential claim. But this does not mean that '*X* is *identifiable*' is mind-involving. Your approach slurs the crucial distinction between actuality and possibility. For consider the pairs: described/describable, mentioned/mentionable, indicated/indicatable, and identified/ identifiable. If one grants that the first member of such a pair is mind-involving, one does not thereby concede that the second member is. Thus, saying that a certain particular is *identified* may well carry a covert reference to a mind, but this does not show that its *identifiability* is mind-dependent. Consequently, since generic particularity demands only identifiability, and not actual identification, your argument that actual identification is mind-involving does not show that *identifiability* is, and so does not suffice to establish the conclusion that particularity is.' So goes the objection. And it is well taken. Its aim is to make the point – a surely correct one – that *actual* identification is not a necessary requirement for being a particular, since there is no contradiction in saying that there are particulars which are not identified (though obviously one cannot give an example of one).

To deal with this objection, let us begin by recognizing the fundamental difference between identification on the one hand, and description, indication, and the rest, on the other. For identification is, in the present context, entirely unique and *sui generis* in a way that impedes straightforward application of the analogy of actual and potential on which the objection rests. It makes perfectly good sense to say of something that is describable but not described or indicatable but not indicated. The actual/ potential distinction is indeed operative in these cases. *But this is not so with identification*: We cannot in principle meaningfully say *of something* that *IT* is identifiable but not identified, because to say this is to commit a literal nonsense. One would be saying explicitly that one doesn't know what one is speaking of. Until it has been identified (however imperfectly) we simply are not dealing with a particular individual thing: we cannot appropriately be held to say anything about 'it' – not even that it is identifiable. To say this is not, of course, to deny that we can speak of otherwise unspecified particulars, as in a statement like 'One of the trees in this forest has treasure buried beneath it.'

But cases of this sort pose no difficulty for our position. Note that (1) if indeed there is treasure under just one tree, then we have, in effect, succeeded in making an identifying reference to it (as 'the tree that has treasure beneath it'); but if there are several trees above a treasure (or none), then there just is no 'it' about which we can be said to be speaking: our purportedly identifying reference fails to refer, and our statement becomes – under these circumstances – semantically unviable.

Consider the following objection: 'It goes without saying that a critical distinction exists between *the thing identified* on the one hand, and on the other *the identification of the thing*. Your argument overlooks this key distinction. Surely, to establish the mind-involvement of the *identification* of the thing does not show the mind-involvement of the thing as such.' This objection hits wide of the mark. It rests on a wholly improper comparison. There is a crucial disanalogy between identifying on the one hand and seeing or describing on the other. For we can only discuss 'the thing identified' once some 'identification of the thing' has been given: *any* consideration of the former (the thing identified) is contingent upon the latter (the identification of the thing). The conceptual viability of 'the thing identified' as an item of consideration is correlative with the identification of the thing at issue. By contrast, nothing whatever about the describability of something rests upon the description of this thing. The hypothetical removal of its identification removes the thing in view in a way that the hypothetical removal of its description would not. This critical disanalogy is fatal for the objection.

But, of course, any such talk of specific things still leaves open the issue of *generic* identifiability. It obviously makes sense to say (generically) that '*Something* is identifiable but not identified' even though it can be admitted that one cannot meaningfully say (specifically) of *something* that IT is identifiable but is not identified. In *this* regard there is a most decisive difference between identification on the one hand and on the other description, ostension, and the rest. And this point is in fact critical for our purposes, because the task of the present discussion is not to maintain merely that the actual identification of particulars is mind-dependent, but that particularity in general is. We must thus confront the *potential* particularity inherent in the claim: '*Something* is identifiable but not identified – though I cannot, of course, tell you what.' Now the viability of this contention was conceded above; and does such a concession not suffice to free that key aspect of particularity at issue in potential identifiability from all ties of mind-dependency?

Not at all. In speaking of 'the identifiable but not identified' we shift to the realm of possibility – of what might or could be, of what is conceivably the case in an area extending beyond that of the actually realized. But *this entire domain of the possible is conceptually mind-involving*, for, as we have already argued at length, the conception of the 'merely' possible is viable only in the context of that of unactualized possibilities, which is fundamentally mind-involving. The upshot of these considerations, then, is that the realm of possibility is as a whole mind-involving, since in falling back from the identi*fied* to the identi*fiable* one is not able to get free of the link of conceptual mind-involvement we have already found operative in the former case.

It should be noted at this point that it is crucially important that we have focussed upon the identifiability and individuatability of particulars, and not, say, upon their *describability* or *perceivability* or the like. To be sure, our argument as to the mind-involvement of possibility in general suffices also to establish the mind-involvement of all these various modes of X-ability. But this argument would in general show only that particulars have a mind-involving feature (describability, perceivability), and so would not cut to the nerve of the issue. If all I know is that some item has a mind-involving feature, the prospect remains open that this feature is but one among many, and that among these others there are also mind-independent ones, so that the item as such is not mind-involving. (In conceding that the color of the apple is mind-involving, the prospect remains that its extension, weight, etc. are not.) Thus in general, the mind-involvement of a feature will not establish the mind-involvement of the thing. But, of course, the story is necessarily otherwise when it is the very *thinghood* – i.e., identifiability or individuatability – of the thing that is at issue. For to establish mind-invocation here is to establish it at a point that touches *the very existence of the item as the item it is.* Once the basic thesis is granted that an experienced particular is individuated as such within the orbit of experience, and is distinguished *intra-experientally* as the item it is, it then follows that we cannot rationally say of IT that it could somehow prove to be independent of mind (given that its very individuality is in essential part the product of mind).

Thus while the general argument that X-ability is mind-invoking – insofar as a reference to unactualized possibilities is involved – suffices to show this also of identifiability or individuatability, we must press the argument one step further. For the key fact is that individuatability is not a somehow incidental feature of a thing but is crucial to its very existence *as an individual thing.* Consequently to show that mind-invocation enters in *at this specific point* is to establish that the very standing of a thing *as the individual particular it is* rests upon a resource the very concept of which involves essential reference to the workings of minds.

To summarize: only two conceptual routes lead into the realm of the particular, that of actual identification and that of potential identifiability. The former, identification, is conceptually mind-invoking because 'to be identified' represents a mind-involving transaction: identification is an attention-directing, and thus a fundamentally mind-invoking process. The latter – identifiability – is mind-involving because the very conception of the possible and potential is at bottom mind-correlative: possibility is *in general* mind-involving, and thus *identifiability* is specifically so.

Thus either way – be it by way of the actual identification of concrete particulars or by way of the conception of identifiable but not identified particulars – one arrives by different roads at the common destination of conceptual mind-invocation.

## 4. A FURTHER ASPECT OF THE MIND-INVOLVEMENT OF 'THINGS'

Yet another aspect of the mind-involvement of the 'things' of our standard view of nature warrants emphasis. Consider, for instance, Descartes' familiar example of a piece of wax – say *that* one. How is one to identify such a thing? Perhaps ostensively as 'that lump of stuff' (pointing). Or perhaps by any of a multiplicity of descriptions: 'that yellow lump in Henry's hand,' or 'the only object in this room with a melting point less than 200° F,' or 'the bit of light substance prepared in such-and-such a way.' That all of these descriptive aspects come together in one and the same thing is, plainly, a *contingent* fact. As Locke held and Hume emphasized, it is certainly a matter of contingent fact that the color, odor, malleability, etc., etc., that characterize the wax all fit together. The self-identical 'thing' that *has* all these attributes, and links them together under the rubric of an established thing-type (a 'lump of wax') is inextricably bound to the *lawful concatenation* of all of these characteristics. Leibniz's idea of things as centers of force and sources of activity, Berkeley's insistence that it is pointless to consider things as apart from the ideas they systematically arouse in us, Kant's theory of the synthesis of apperception constitutive of our thing-concepts, Mill's idea of physical objects as 'permanent possibilities of sensation,' Lotze's conception of things as the product of laws, all point to a common destination: the fact that the concrete 'things' of nature, on our standard view of the matter, are only identifiable through the lawfulness of their 'effects,' and that the very concept of a physical object, on our standard conception, calls for a reference to laws. The mere unity of a particular as the item it is is law-constituted. If something we held to be an apple did not suitably 'behave as an apple' – if on the inside it were leaden, or if it looked triangular from above, etc., etc. – then we simply could not maintain the claim that it was an apple. The 'thinghood' of a natural particular as it figures in our conceptual scheme turns on its sortal nature, and is accordingly only to be comprehended in lawful and so ultimately possibilistic (and dispositional) terms. And this inevitably brings modes of lawfulness upon the scene. It is a pivotal consideration for us, as for Kant, that the conception of a particular – and especially of a material object – is fundamentally law-involving.

On our standard conception, things can only be specified in terms that render them correlative with laws and inconceivable without them. And given this crucial fact of law-correlativity, our earlier analysis of the conceptual mind-involvingness of law-fulness suffices to establish that of thinghood as well.

Though I regard this line of argument as perfectly adequate to make the point at issue, I have given it a subordinate place in the discussion only because it presents the case in a more circuitous way, relying crucially upon *several* earlier stages of the argument. In casting the thesis that lawfulness is mind-involving as a conceded premiss, it drives us back to the complex process by which this thesis was argued.[4]

## 5. THE ROLE OF MIND APPRAISED

Our thesis that particularity is mind-involving is not, of course, a *factual* contention regarding the particulars of this actual world. It is a *conceptual* thesis to the general effect that, given the way in which the relevant concepts (particularity, identifia-bility, and the rest) function in the conceptual scheme that is their natural home, a certain result – viz., that particularity is an inherently mind-involving conception – must obtain.

This position can be illuminated from a variant point of view. It is possible and plausible to hold that *thinghood* hinges on the identification of particulars and that particular identification invariably requires some descriptive machinery, that is, some sortal classifiers.[5] But now, if (as we shall subsequently argue) the descriptive machinery we employ itself hinges on a con-tingently held conceptual framework, then it at once follows that the mind can in principle divide nature into *things* (particulars) in potentially different ways. It will accordingly happen – at least over a wide range – that how we proceed to inventory 'observed reality' into different things may depend upon our

---

[4] Someone might be tempted to reason as follows: 'Material things are theoretical constructs; and this theory-dependence renders them mind-dependent.' But this line of thought would imply, quite erroneously, that we cannot have theories about mind-independent things. On our view, the mind-involvement of natural particulars inheres NOT in *that* they are objects of theory BUT in *how* they are objects of theory, viz., in such a way that the theory stipulates their possession of lawful aspects.

[5] See David Wiggins, *Identity and Spatio-Temporal Continuity* (New York, 1967).

culture, our interests, or the like. What constitutes a particular unit may vary drastically: nothing, for example, precludes us from taking as one single unit an auto plus its passengers plus its contents. In sum, how we go about sorting observed reality into units is *partially* arbitrary (i.e., naturally underdetermined)[6] to an extent that invariably calls for mental intervention of a decisional act. Identity on this view is a framework-relative concept of the presupposition-involving type. Many conceptions obviously involve others by way of presupposition, as society presupposes *agency* or price *exchange* or the looks of things *vision*. So too identity, on the present view, requires a *framework* of identification[7] as its perhaps not wholly obvious presupposition – and the standard framework for the manifest objects of our nature is replete with mind-invoking conceptions.

From this angle, too, particularity is mind-invoking, because not only is individuation as such a mind-involving process, but the specific identificatory mechanisms we standardly use in the specification of particulars are – so we maintain– throughout laden with mind-invoking conceptions.[8]

It appears, moreover, that Leibniz was right in regarding mind-endowed persons as the paradigm particulars, so that the concept of thinghood in general is patterned on something accessible in first-hand experience. But the following objection arises here:

On this Leibnizian position adopted here, mind is not only

[6] If an adequate theory of nature were given by an Atomism on the lines of that of the Ancient Greeks, this indeterminedness of observed, manifest thinghood might cease at the microlevel. But the microobjects of modern physics are so nonstandard that the concept of a *thing* scarcely seems applicable here at all.

[7] Given this view of *identity* as a framework-relative conception, it follows that there are no absolute, purely independent and objective things in some metaphysically categorical mode. The result is something of a Leibnizian monadology without monads, i.e., with all individuals as *phaenomena*-more-or-less-*bene-fundata*.

[8] For example, we generally identify physical particulars on the basis of their *effects* (observable and other) that is, on the basis of their dispositions to produce certain results. And as we saw above, such dispositional characterizations are inherently mind-invoking.

a natural particular but even a *paradigmatic* particular providing something of a model for our conception of particularity.
But how can one coherently view minds as particulars if
particularity is – as argued above – mind-invoking.

The answer to this problem lies in noting that two quite different
sorts of mind-involvingness are at issue. The particularity of minds
is – obviously – not mind-made, but is clearly something *overtly*
mind-referential. And the particularity of other, nonmentalistic
things, though not itself overtly mentalistic in nature, is constituted on a mental paradigm. Thus the seeming circularity of
the position is removed by drawing the necessary distinctions.


## 6. SOME OBJECTIONS

But what can one say to the objector who in the name of
'common sense' protests: 'Surely all this is wild eccentricity. The
existence of particular objects does not require the existence of
minds. The moon would certainly exist even if there were no
minds and never had been (although then, of course, no one
would be *aware* of its existence).' In a way this is all quite right –
but only in a way. The key question is just *what* it would be that
would exist. It won't do to reply 'the moon' – such proper
names have to be cashed in: only what has *previously* been
identified can be named.[9] But what is this 'moon' at issue here?
Certainly it wouldn't be the moon as we conceive of it (as the

---

[9] The point is that naming – like labelling but unlike identifying – is not
a procedure for introducing new items upon the stage of discussion. To
label an object, we must already have it in view, and similarly with
naming. Thus when something is named, this presupposes that its individuation or identification has already been completed. From the
theoretical standpoint, a name is like a relative pronoun: it affords a
conveniently abbreviated mode of reference to something already
introduced before. To say this is not to deny that we can name something not yet actually extant (e.g., a ship that as yet 'exists only in the
minds of its planners'). But, of course, the identity of the so-named item
is already established in terms of various linkages to extant things (the
planners and their plans). Examples of this sort do not invalidate our
thesis that identification is conceptually prior to naming (though actual
existence need certainly not be so).

largest natural satellite of the earth, the celestial body celebrated in endless romantic songs, the planetary object visited by Messrs Aldrin, Armstrong, and Collins, etc.). The pivotal point is the near-trivial remark that *concepts* are used in all carving up of reality into distinguishable particulars (the moon included). *Antecedently*, in order to effect a completed individuation, a mind-involving process of conceptualization is always necessary to provide the requisite identificatory framework. Now, of course, once the identification is effected, there need be nothing *further* that is mind-dependent about the item. Thus *consequently*, from this post-identification standpoint, it is perfectly acceptable to say that 'the moon would exist if there were no minds to be aware of its existence.' But such a concession of *identification-consequent* mind-independence does not militate against our thesis of a *fundamental* identification-coordinated mind-dependence of particulars. A world in which this process of mind-invoking conceptualization itself is hypothesized to be *aufgehoben* is one in which its results – particulars included – must be given up as well. It is a world in which there might generically be *existence* but to which the idea of particular *existents* would be inapplicable.[10]

Another objection deserves notice. Someone might argue 'How can you say that particulars are mind-constituted, when there certainly were particular things in the universe prior to the evolution of minds: dinosaurs, for example.' This objection misses the point entirely. The issue is not one of natural history: ours is a *conceptual* and not an *historical* conclusion. To say that a cloud is fish-like is to characterize it in mind-involving terms ('looks like a fish' – and *looks* are clearly mind-referring), but this is not to say that there might perfectly well have been fish-like clouds before the evolution of minds (or of fish, for that matter). Caesar could very well have had some Napoleonic traits of personality. There is no reason why a concept cannot be projected backwards to a point of history prior to the existence of the frame of reference from which it draws its meaning – but

[10] Here, of course, the issue is not one of just *whose* minds are to be assumed to be absent, but of the inapplicability of certain essentially mind-referential concepts.

this fact does not free it from conceptual dependence upon this frame of reference. (Cf. the discussion of point (2) on pp. 21–22 above.)

A related, but more subtle objection can be put as follows:

> We must bear in mind the fundamental contrast between the *invention* of something new and the *discovery* of something preexisting. Your conceptualistic theory of particularity takes the first route, but why should the second be excluded? Why should we not take the view that when the mind individuates something, then this is simply the *recognition* by it of an item that was there 'before' this individuation (in a conceptual sense), and whose individuation confirms rather than creates its individuality?

The reply lies in paying careful heed to the question: What is this 'it' of which we can supposedly say correctly that its identity antecedes its identification? Of course once something is identified then we can, *ex post facto*, claim its preexistence. Once identifications are in hand, and we know whereof we talk, then, from *within* the domain of post-identificatory considerations we can, of course, adopt the language of discovery and preexistence. It is only when we raise *external* questions regarding this domain itself that the issue of the conceptual mechanisms of identification itself becomes crucial.

### 7. OUR VIEW NOT IMMATERIALISM

One key point must be reemphasized. We are not maintaining that reality is spiritual (let alone that only spirits are real). The present discussion does not support immaterialism. The matrix of reality within which mind operates to effect its discrimination of individuals may – for all that the present discussion establishes – be as material as can be. To be sure, we maintain that mind plays an essential role in the *constitution* of distinct and differentiated things (i.e., particulars). But the constitutive role of mind here is such as to make the emphasis fall upon the *distinctness* rather than the *things*, or – perhaps better – upon its thing-status rather than the thing itself.

We are not saying that 'ultimate reality' – whatever this may be – is mental, but rather that the cutting-up of our real world into particular individual things is an inevitably mind-involving transaction. In speaking somewhat figuratively (though by no means improperly) of the mind's creation of real particulars, it is in fact not their reality but their particularity or individuality that is viewed as mind-derived on the present approach. It is not *reality* but *thinghood* that is inherently mentalistic according to our argument. The key factor of mind-involvement enters in *via* the conceptual mechanisms through which alone the identification of specific things and the distinction between them come about. It would be misleading to say of these things simply that *they* are mind-created.

While our position is not spiritualistic, and does not hold that natural particulars are somehow physically constituted *of* minds (or 'mental stuff'), it does hold that they are conceptually constituted *by* minds. And going even beyond this, it seems not implausible to view that mind-endowed physical complex the *person* itself as the paradigm particular. For insofar as *separateness* of identity and *continuity* of existence (i.e., self-identity through change) are crucial elements of our concept of an individual, a particular thing, the idea of person is eminently qualified to serve as model. It is here, at the level of first-hand experience of persons, that we seemingly have our most firmly based and experientially familiar contact with particularity. In this perspective the concept of particularity appears not only as mind-dependent but even as mind-patterned.

We grant and indeed insist upon the incontrovertible truism that mind creates not things but the *ideas* of things. But this very dictum has a special bearing upon particulars. Any particular upon the stage of discussion or consideration is *constituted* as the thing it is by answering to its identifying idea. The mind does not *create* things but *conceives* them by its deployment of the conceptual mechanisms by which alone the concept of particularity can find application. Even if reality 'is wholly material' and all things are 'made up of matter' the carving-up of the all-inclusive pie into *particular* things is, and cannot but be, the work of mind. Mind is thus essential not to the 'physical' but to the *conceptual* constitution of particular things. This position thus adheres in a duly qualified manner to the thesis of Kant and the Husserl of the *Cartesian Meditations* that the mind constitutes the objects of knowledge. This constituting is not, however, a matter of the causal *creation* of things but of their conceptual *organization*, of providing the specific modes of unitary itemhood that are deployed in the rational structuring of our experiencing of the world. It is in this organizational sense alone – and not that of *causal* genesis – that we wish to argue for the mind-relatedness of physical particulars.

## 8. THE PROBLEM OF 'THE THING IN ITSELF'

It is useful to look at the matter of mind-independent reality from a Kantian perspective. A starting point is provided by the thesis that:

> The basic concepts in terms of which we standardly think of the things of this world – regarding them as material particulars, located in space and time, and interacting causally – are all mind-involving.

On this beginning, it is tempting to think of a framework of natural things somehow constituting a mind-independent reality behind the phenomenal surface – a reality composed of things corresponding to those of our manifest experience, but possessed only of 'objective,' mind-independent features. Accordingly, someone might be tempted to object along the following lines:

> What you say regarding the mind-dependency of particulars may well hold true of 'the objects of ordinary experience,' but certainly not of the *objects of science*.

This objection carries us back to a dualism of the type made notorious by Eddington.[11] According to such a view, over and above the thought of the chair, *via* the thoughts various persons have of it (which is *obviously* and trivially mind-dependent), there is

[11] A. S. Eddington, *The Nature of the Physical World* (Cambridge and New York, 1928), pp. ix–x.

(1) the chair-as-we-think-of-it under the aegis of a certain identifying description that 'introduces it into discussion (or consideration)': '*that* chair (pointing),' 'grandfather's favorite seat,' 'the largest piece of furniture in the room.'

(2) the chair *an sich*, as it exists in itself, apart from any specific conception of it.

This line of thought leads to the conception of a plurality of things-in-themselves (*Dinge an sich*) corresponding to the ordinary things of everyday experience. We arrive at a position that postulates a plurality of real things in *correlation* with the plurality of manifest things. Such things-in-themselves are viewed as duly co-ordinated with the standard things of ordinary experience.

This position is untenable because item (2), the *an sich* particular freed of all traces of mind-dependency, does not represent a viable idea. It is not merely an 'idealization,' but an altogether unrealistic one. Just as a building cannot be seen *an sich* independently of *every* perspective (though it is, of course, independent of *any* perspective), so the chair cannot be conceived *an sich* as apart from any and every specific identificatory conception of it. In considering the chair we are thus reduced to item (1) which is a conception-involving (and so thought involving) hybrid. Clearly any explication of what is at issue with respect to the-chair-as-we-conceive-of-it involves a reference to our standard conceptualization of the chair, and is accordingly conceptually mind-involving, given the nature of the conceptual framework within which our standard conceptualization is deployed.

Of course, this position still leaves open the concept of one single all-embracing, and so distinction-free, generic physical reality, a monolithic reality-in-general without a diversified multiplicity of real particulars: a monistic realm of *the thing-in-itself* (*das Ding an sich*) without a pluralism of *things in themselves* (*Dinge an sich*). Here one arrives at a domain of capital-R Reality characterized by the essentially negative feature that whatever can be said of it truly must be said in wholly mind-independent terms. This may be a somewhat dark and problematic notion, and more will be said about it below. But our analysis

I

does enable us to carry away immediately the one small fact that Reality (in this generic and mind-independent sense) – while conceivably qualifying as a particular itself – certainly does not include particulars, and thus highlights from another perspective one aspect of Bradley's dictum that 'the Absolute is not many; there are no independent reals.'[12] The key fact is that this mind-independent 'absolute' is a world without particulars: a 'night in which all cows are black.' The removal of the mind-invoking element leaves no room for the distinctness of individually distinguishable things.

On the view set out here, the-chair-as-I-think-of-it simply could not exist as such (that is, *as* I think of it) in a 'mindless' setting freed of all mind-invoking terms of reference, since the terms in which I do and cannot but think of it – as a particular item of a certain sort located in space and time, causally interlinked with other things and endowed with various law-governed potentialities – are in general in some respect mind-invoking. (It is certainly not the case that I think of the chair itself as somehow mind-involving in some panpsychistic or spiritualistic manner – any more than I need to think of an imagined or hallucinated elephant as being imagined or hallucinated.[13])

But even if one grants that things-as-we-think-of-them are con-

---

[12] F. H. Bradley, *Appearance and Reality* (2nd ed., Oxford, 1930), p. 127. We shall return to this conception of 'a world without particulars' in Chapter X. However, one thing needs to be set straight right away. If the all-embracing, totalistic cosmic-absolute that comprehends all of natural reality is accepted as 'a particular thing,' then our thesis of the mind-dependence of particularity needs to be qualified at just this point. For it revolves about the requisite for concepts and criteria in the drawing of thing-separating distinctions, and there is no distinguishing to be done here. Thus at this one, somewhat extreme, point an exception to our thesis that particularity is conceptually mind-dependent may become mandatory, but can indeed be made here without any damage to the over-all argument.

[13] Recall the previous distinction between constitutive and regulative features of the objects of thought. What renders an item mind-involving is not the possession of some mind-invoking features, but having some that are essential to it as such. It is in *this* sense that the natural particulars that compose the-world-as-we-think-of-it (on the common conceptual scheme) are fundamentally mind-involving.

ceived of in terms heavily endowed with mind-invoking features (and in particular that they are identified through descriptive mechanisms that are both mind-constituted and mind-referring) could one not nevertheless, form the idea of a *nondescript* something corresponding to the item in question, a *Ding-an-sich*? The answer here is No, but a No that needs explanation and qualification.

When one attempts the intellectual exercise of beginning with the-chair-as-I-think-of-it and then stripping this of all those features here categorized as mind-involving, then what one is left with – whatever it may be – is certainly no longer *this* chair. We may be left with a generic something-or-other, but the specific particular with which we began has been lost. Just this is the burden of argument that particularity is mind-dependent. We must face up to the implications of the fact there simply is no viable way of getting at *the object that* is cognized (seen) except through the mediation of *the object as* it is cognized. There is, in the final analysis, nothing we can know or say of the former save what is accessible to us under the aegis of the latter. If we are pressed hard here we would fall back on some variation of the Lockean theme of *je ne sais quoi*.

The argument against the conception of a particular *Ding an sich* corresponding to a specific manifest object must be indicated in greater detail. The basic premiss of the argument is the thesis that we identify each particular manifest object of the world about us from the vantage point of a conceptual perspective. This perspectival aspect is the key. For note that it would be quite senseless to say 'I want to know how the room looks, looks actually and objectively, not just from this or that perspective but really "in itself".' To say this would be nonsense because the *looks* of a room can only be presented perspectivally. And analogously, according to our view the *identity* of a particular can only be specified perspectivally: its identity, and so *it itself* as the specific individual it is, is perspective-restricted. To talk about 'what this chair *really* is' as apart from this or that conceptual (and so on our view mind-invoking) perspective – not under this or that specific identification but 'objectively and in itself' – is misguided, since the chair can itself only be specified relative to a framework of identification. And insofar as this framework is mind-involving, so also is individuation, and the idea of a specific and mind-independent individual – a particular thing-in-itself – is unworkable.

We certainly can in Kantian fashion adopt the idea of a *Ding an sich* to serve in a *regulative* manner as a contrast with the manifest particulars of common experience. But we must distinguish here between three concepts, those of (1) one overarching archetypal something, *das Ding an sich* (2) an otherwise undifferentiated plurality of *Dinge an sich* as a sort of night in which all cows are black (though there may well be a plurality of them), (3) a plurality of *Dinge an sich* corresponding to the differentiated particulars of the world of our experience, each manifest thing having an *an sich* counterpart correlative to itself. Now our position is only that the *Ding an sich* of type (3) is untenable. The fact that particularity and specificity require a mind-involving element of identification precludes anything of the *an sich* (and so *ex hypothesi* mind-independent) variety from being of this type.

# Chapter VII

# THE MIND-DEPENDENCY OF TIME AND SPACE

## PART I: TIME

### 1. THE THESIS

The present chapter will argue a thesis that is bound to seem strange at first sight, namely that space and time are mind-dependent. Hopefully, the considerations to be adduced will succeed in mitigating some of this initial strangeness. Certainly the flat statement of the contention is only a poor beginning – it remains thoroughly unhelpful until distinctions are drawn and explanations given. These latter tasks present the principal objective.

### 2. AN OBJECTION

An immediate refutation of the view that time is mind-dependent can plausibly be attempted by means of the following seemingly straightforward argument:

1. To say that time is mind-dependent is to say (*inter alia*) that if there were no minds there would be no time.
2. But if there were no time there would be no change, since the very concept of change involves that of time.
3. Therefore if there were no minds there would be no change, which is absurd.[1]

---

[1] Essentially this very argument to establish via the reality of change the thesis that time itself must be real is criticized in the *Critique of Pure Reason* by Kant, who formulates it as follows: 'Alterations are real, this being proved by change of our own representations – even if all outer appearances, together with their alterations, be denied. Now alterations are possible only in time, and time is therefore something real' (A37, B53).

It is thus argued that since the conclusion is patently unaccept-able, any philosophical theory which makes no provision for change and the variation of occurrences outside the sphere of the mental being thereby so paradoxical as to be untenable. I am pre-pared to accept this contention and do not wish to quarrel with it. But once this concession has been made, it is then asserted that the unacceptability of the conclusion recoils upon the first premiss since – so it is said – the second premiss is uncontestable. The argument is thus presented as a decisive refutation of the mind-dependency of time. However, the springing of this trap does not in actual fact close it upon its prey. A way of bypassing these obstacles can be found by noting some crucial distinctions that reveal the serious vulnerability of the second premiss.

### 3. FULL-BLOODED TIME VS. BARE TEMPORALITY

Our ordinary and somewhat loosely structured concept of 'time' represents a constellation of ideas ranging from what may be con-ceived of as a bare minimum conception of *temporality* to an enhanced and more full-blooded concept of *time* proper. Bare temporality has two basic conceptual constituents:

(1) the conception of different occasions or junctures at which varying states of affairs obtain. (I shall label this the postulate of *occasion diversity*.)

(2) the conception that these different occasions or junctures fall into a one-dimensional sequential ordering of earlier/ simultaneous with/later. (I shall label this the postulate of *occasion ordinality*.)

It should be noted that the terminology of 'junctures' or 'occa-sions' rather than of 'times' or 'moments' (= moments *of time*) is used here in a quasi-technical sense to avoid prejudging the issue by question-begging implications that time is already bodily present in full panoply upon the stage of consideration.

The move from such austere *prototemporality* to the more ambitious conception of *time proper* involves the addition of two further conceptual components:

(3) the conception that the different junctures at issue fall not merely into the sequential ordering of a dating-scheme but into a *measurable* structure for which *chronometry* is possible. (I shall label this as the postulate of *occasion cardinality* or shall also speak of it as that of *temporal measurability*.)

(4) the introduction of the concept of 'the present' – i.e., of 'now' as one characteristically outstanding juncture.[2] (I shall label this as the postulate of *occasion presentness* and shall also speak of it – for reasons soon to be explained – as that of *temporal interiorization*.)

Only by adding to the concept of bare or minimal temporality these two factors of measurability and presentness do we move to the fully articulated idea of time as such. These facets of time must be considered in greater detail.

The addition of occasion-presentness (i.e., nowness) to the machinery of mere temporality enables us to move from the occasion ordinality of what McTaggart calls the B-series which orders moments into earlier/simultaneous with/later to arrive at what he calls the A-series of

past = earlier than *now*
present = now = simultaneous with *now*
future = later than *now*.

Our perspective reflects the now-classical position of McTaggart's *The Nature of Existence*[3] namely his emphasis upon the critical difference between the mere occasion ordinality of the B-series (earlier/simultaneous/later) and the now-relative fully temporal specification of the A-series (past/present/future). With the A-series we supplement the generic idea of a temporally successive sequence of occasions essential to bare temporality by the *interior* point of view of a definite place ('now') *within* the series.

[2] Regarding the crucial role of this now-of-the-present in the articulation of the concept of time see N. Rescher and A. Urquhart, *Temporal Logic* (Vienna and New York, 1971).

[3] Cambridge, 1921. For a commentary see C. D. Broad, *An Examination of McTaggart's Philosophy* (3 vols., Cambridge, 1933–8). For an interesting treatment see Richard Gale, *The Philosophy of Time* (New York, 1967).

With the B-series one takes the external point of view of Olympian detachment; with the A-series one is placed *in medias res*, one takes an internal stance *within* the sequence of events. Temporality rests on *external*, time on *internal* comparisons that must be made from a vantage-point within the framework. Bare temporality is thus merely the (indispensable) starting-point from which we only reach the full-blooded complexity of the concept of time after due supplementation.

Now, bare temporality is all that is needed to establish the basic concept of change. The B-series machinery of a temporal sequence of succession with different states of affairs obtaining at different junctures is quite enough to supply the needed foothold: all that is requisite for change in the minimal sense of alteration in the state of things is bare temporality; full blooded time is not needed. The mere differences are enough to establish the fact of change – the further ramifications of their full temporal context need not be appealed to.

The second premiss of the preceding argument thus collapses. It is not *time* as such but *temporality*, in the somewhat technical sense at issue here, that is indispensable for change. For time goes beyond mere temporality in two respects: internalization and measuration. Indeed time proper might be characterized as *the measure of change from within*, that is from a perspective interior to the course of change itself.

On this view, our standard concept of 'time' is a complex or *constellation* of ideas ranging from (1) the minimal conception of temporality (which can be viewed in the B-series perspective sufficient for change) to (2) the full blooded conception of time-proper as involving the A-series perspective of internal positioning together with a concept of chronometry (i.e., temporal metrization.) The drawing of these distinctions serves to invalidate the second premiss of the counterargument with which we began.

### 4. THE MIND-DEPENDENCY OF TIME (I.E., FULL-BLOODED TIME)

Having rejected the claim that change requires time (a premiss essential to the given objection to our thesis) by suitably distinguishing between basic temporality and more complexly full-blooded time, we can now turn to our major task: the argument for the mind-dependency of time. In building up our case here, we shall argue the mind-dependency not of basic *temporality* but of *time proper*. Specifically, the discussion will endeavor to maintain the mind-dependency of nowness or presentness, the key factor in distinguishing bare temporality from time proper.

In outline, our argument is this. The occasion diversity and occasion ordinality of bare temporality are not seen as mind-dependent save in the minimal sense of a conceptual mind-invokingness, in that the identification of *particular* occasions is called for. For clearly, the specification of particular occasions must proceed through that of the particular events that differentiate it from others, and this calls for acts of individuation that fall within the strictures of the preceding chapter. Moreover, the measurability aspect of full-blooded time is no more than conceptually mind-involving (in ways shortly to be examined). But the aspect of nowness and presentness of full-blooded time does bring minds upon the stage of consideration in such a way that an outright mind-dependency results. Let us turn to a more detailed scrutiny of these issues.

## (1) *Measurability*

The *measurability* of time is a distinctive factor additional to the mere ordinality of basic temporality. A plurality of different moments in succession is far from enough to provide for a measurable time. A succession could be altogether chaotic and disorganized, whereas a very high degree of order is required for chronometry, the observational measurement of time: primarily the existence of duly correlated periodic processes. There is certainly the possibility of temporality – and so of *change* – without the high degree of orderliness needed for capital-T Time. But a world in which *chronometry* is to be possible – a world in which periodic processes can be used as basis for the actual measurement of change – must possess a high degree of internal order and constitute a *lawful* world. (Our dreams, for example, involve succession and so temporality, but lack the internal lawfulness requisite for time proper.)

The operations of chronometric measurement are possible only in a setting where a great many laws of the form 'if one were to do . . ., then observational result would be . . .' are operative. The operation of natural laws is essential to underwrite chronometry, and this brings time proper within the sphere of our analysis of the mind-dependency of lawfulness. For at this point our line of argument clearly falls back into a previous train of ideas. Thus if chronometry is only possible in a world subject to a suitable framework of natural laws, and if lawfulness is mind-involving – as we have already argued at length – then time proper (i.e., a full-blooded time that calls for measurability) is also mind-involving.

There is yet another aspect of mind-involvement present in that temporal mensuration characterized as chronometry. Observational mensuration of *all* sorts – the chronometric included – requires the specification of concrete individuals, and calls for their identification and indeed reidentification: it is crucial that in the measuring process we deal at each given stage with one self-same measuring implement, with *the same* measuring rod or *the same* clock (or other periodic mechanism). And, of course, such *reidentification* demands and indeed surpasses the demand for the identification of particulars. Thus if our case for the mind-involvement of particular-identification has any merit, it works also to establish the mind-involvement of mensuration in general and chronometry in particular.

## (2) *Presentness*

We now turn to *presentness*, the second key aspect of full-blooded time. As observed above, A-series time requires the specifying of a particular 'now' to supplement the general machinery of B-series precedence. This calls for the specification from within the course of temporal events of a certain outstanding juncture, the present 'now'. The 'now-of-the-present' as a particular 'moment of time' requires an explicit *act of awareness* for its identification. It is clear that this identificatory distinguishing of one particular moment of time is of the same order as particular-identification in general but has the feature that it can only be accomplished in an ostensive way, i.e., by an experience. Only on the basis of a participatory engagement within the sequence of events *in medias res* can a certain specific moment of time be distinguished as 'the present.' The presentness of the now is of its very nature an *experiential* presentness, and this fact renders it overtly mind-involving. (And derivatively, communication about temporal matters requires the connecting linkage of *common* experiences, and accordingly endows time with an inherently social dimension.)

On this view, full-blooded time (unlike bare temporality) is not merely conceptually mind-invoking, but is outright mind-dependent, because the essential factor of presentness introduces an overt reference to an experiencing mind into the analysis of what is at issue. Here it is not just a matter of deploying concepts which (like those of lawfulness or particularity) are conceptually mind-invoking, in that their full analysis requires some ultimate recourse to concepts whose adequate explication brings out the covert and framework-internal role of mentalistic processes. Rather, the conception of nowness is such that its immediate definitional analysis brings to light an overt reference to mentalistic processes of experiencing in such a way as to establish outright mind-dependency.

In medieval philosophical usage, now (*nunc*) represented simply a moment of time (not necessarily *the present* one); accordingly, it made sense to distinguish *a* now (i.e., an instant) from *the* now (i.e., the *present* instant, the now-of-the-present). But, of course, presentness cries out for a recipient, to be present is to be present *to someone*. With 'now' (the *real* now, i.e., the now-of-the-present) one comes up against the critical difference between 'at *a* juncture' and 'at *this* juncture.' And here, as always, the ostensive identificatory 'this' presupposes an apprehending intelligence bringing with it the awareness indispensable to any identificatory transaction. The very concept of the now-of-the-present is thus inseparably linked with a conscious experience, the experience of a being who, from a position of placement within the framework of temporality assumes with conscious awareness that temporal *perspective* through which alone the A-series distinctions of past/present/future can come into operation. Such an intellectual perspective can alone transmute the B-series relationships of temporality into a full-blooded order of time deployed about a pivotal *now*. The A-series relations are inherently mind-involving because they presuppose temporalized experience: the present experienced, the past remembered, the future anticipated. It is this experiential involvement of full-blooded time (A-series time) that is the basis of its mind-dependence. Temporality (i.e., B-series time) is of itself an insufficient foundation for this mind-requiring generation of full-blooded time itself.

It is (or should be) obvious that a conceptual point is at issue here, and that the transition from temporality to time is not a stage of natural history. We are *not* saying 'At first there was only temporality and then with the evolution of minds time proper came into being.' Once again, the issue is not one of historical development but of the nature of the conceptual resources needed for the adequate exposition of the components of a certain concept. It is an analytical and not a causal dependence on mind that is operative in this discussion.

\* \* \*

The given line of reasoning, however, serves to show only that *time* (i.e., proper time) is mind-dependent, not that *temporality* is. Assume – to the contrary of our position – that McTaggart's own view were correct and that there can be no B-series without an A-series, i.e., that succession inherently admits of interiorization. This view, which I do not share, would force the present line of argument to the conclusion that *all change* would be mind-dependent. If McTaggart's teaching *were* correct, then the mind-dependency of time would infect temporality as well. This, of course, leads at once to the view that if 'objective reality' excludes all traces of mind-dependency, then time and temporality and their congeners are all alike 'unreal.' Essentially this is McTaggart's position. I need not repeat at this point why I think it to be wrong. Our position is exactly the Leibnizian one that time is a 'well founded phenomenon,' in that mind-independent temporality provides the foundation for mind-dependent time. Time proper is 'phenomenal' through the element of mind-dependency: it is 'well founded' by having as its basis a temporality that is no more than conceptually mind-invoking.

## 5. SOME OBJECTIONS

The mind-dependency of Time has been maintained by a long series of philosophers of very varied tradition. In this regard the views of Leibniz, the British Idealists, Henri Bergson, and William James are too well known to need restatement here. In recent years the mind-dependence of time has been argued with great learning and acuteness by Adolf Grünbaum, and eloquently defended by him against a host of critics. Grünbaum does not base his position on the sorts of conceptual considerations adduced here, but argues – effectively by elimination – that nowness is mentalistic because it is not *physically* real, since the idea of 'the present' plays no role whatever in physical theory:

Apart from its minor usage to designate an arbitrarily chosen event of reference in the Minkowski diagram, the term 'now' functions as an anthropocentric designation whose referent is mind-dependent; what is 'now' about a physical event is that some of its immediate effects *are conceptualized as being presented* to the conscious *awareness* of one or more (human) perceivers. And if a (human or other conceptualizing) perceiver proceeds to express that awareness in a linguistic utterance, the quasi-simultaneity of the physical event with that utterance is an indicator of the nowness of the physical event in question. Thus, in the first instance, nowness is an attribute of experienced events which are being *consciously* registered and conceptualized as occurring, and the awareness of this now-content can coincide with an awareness of other events as remembered and of still others as envisioned. Psychological or common-sense time is constituted by the ordered diversity of the 'now-contents' of conscious awareness, these now-contents being ordered with respect to the relations 'earlier than' and 'later than'. Hence, the *diversity* of the now-contents allows us to regard as a fact the 'now' of conceptualizing awareness. But if this factual statement is not to turn into a tautology, the transciency of the 'now' must be understood as mere diversity, that is, as directionally neutral with respect to the past and the future.[4]

Physical theory talks in the timeless present of pure mathematics. In its pursuit of general truths it abstracts from all particularity, and so cannot recognize some outstandingly present juncture as the *now*. Such presentness is fundamentally *experiental* and relates inherently to an *awareness* of given content of which physics from its Olympianly synoptic perspective can take no differentially specific cognizance no more than the universal-minded God of Aristotle could take note of the accidental vagaries of concrete particulars. The failure of science to deal as such with a differentiated past, present, and future (i.e., A-series time) is paradigmatic of its objectivity: its aversion to ego-centricity is manifested in a refusal to assume *any* particularistic points of view – *I/my*, *here*, and *now* all falling into the juris-diction of this self-denying ordinance. The exclusion of A-series time is accordingly typical of the insistence of theoretical science upon universalistic generality.

Various arguments have been urged against Grünbaum's view, many of which have in fact been dealt with here at one place or another. However, one particularly beguiling counterargument has been presented by Frederick Ferré:

. . . our minds are no less part of the natural order than our bodies. . . . But the phenomenological fact is that for subjective awareness some mental events [viz., the *present* ones] are uniquely 'favored' over others (in the sense of being judged 'now'). Thus a systemati-cally incoherent division is created between the order of *mental events* conceived as occurring tenselessly, on the one hand, in a per-fect democracy of earlier-later relations wherein none has special occurring transiently, on the other hand, in a remorselessly ruled public succession of present moments.[5]

Ferré's point seems to be the argument: If (1) physics views all

[4] Adolf Grünbaum, 'The Anisotropy of Time' in T. Gold and D. L. Schu-macher (eds), *The Nature of Time* (Ithaca, 1967).

[5] Frederick Ferré, 'Grünbaum vs. Dobbs: The Need for Physical Tran-siency,' *British Journal for the Philosophy of Science*, vol. 21 (1970), pp. 278–80.

moments of time as wholly alike, and (2) the mind gives to one moment, the 'present' one, an experiential preeminence, then how can physics possibly explain *this* mental phenomenon. Hence one must either insist – all indications to the contrary notwithstanding – that physics *does* recognize a preeminent 'now,' or one must give up the thesis that physics can account for mental phenomena in general. But this objection misses fire. Let it be that pure (and so strictly theoretical) physics treats all moments alike. But that does not mean that, *given* any moment, then from *its* temporal perspective physics cannot regard other moments in a highly nonuniform way, and specifically cannot yield from the vantage point of *this* time a certain preeminence and primary significance (relative to this given time) to those events occurring *at that time.* Thus *relative* to a given experimental juncture the events occurring 'now' (i.e., *then*) can indeed enjoy a special and prime status. But there is nothing in *this* (essentially transtemporal) fact that means that a physics which 'treats all times as on a par' cannot explain mental occurrences, such as the feeling of 'experiential presence' relative to contemporary occurrences, which we experience *at the time* (but indeed experience, at *all* times that we are conscious, relative to *then*-observed occurrences). Physics need not and cannot find in *this* experience of nowness a certain characteristic 'presentness' generically different from other experience of nowness. And that it cannot do so is not a defect at all; physical theory can perfectly well maintain – without creating any absurdity – that different moments do not differ in *nowness* at all rather than merely in their corresponding occurences, that is, in *content.* The fact of 'experiential presentness' as such is common to all successive moments in the life of the conscious being, as a special relationship between thenoccurrent observations and the then-occurrent 'state of mind' towards certain occurences – viz., that they are 'uniquely present.' What is different at these different times is not the consciousness of being present (= nowness) at all, but simply what is going on: not consciousness but experienced content, and at this level physical explanation is unquestionably feasible. Physics need not, nay should not, be saddled with the (from its own standpoint essentially impossible) mission of finding some unique feature of the present 'now' that differentiates it from the 'nows' of other moments of time.

On our view, no characteristic feature unique to time *per se* is at issue in this connection. The mind-dependence of the now is seen as part of a very general phenomenon, viz., the mind-involvement of every facet of *experiential* particularity. From this perspective, the failure of pure, theoretical science to take cognizance of 'the present' is seen as wholly of a piece with its not taking cognizance of other experientially determined particulars. The concrete particulars we do or can encounter in the orbit of experience do, of course, fall under the generalizations of pure science – what physics teaches us of time-in-general must hold of 'the present' and what biology attributes to man-in-general will hold of you and me. But such particulars as we come to identify on the basis of experiential encounter do not *as such* enter into the sphere of pure science. This feature – its 'abstraction' from all experientially encountered particularity – is the basis for the abstention of pure science from cognizance of the now-of-the-present and its cognate involvement with a full blooded time of past, present, and future.[6] Unlike the deliverances of our personal experience, science is altogether standpoint-neutral.

Consider another objection closely related to the preceding one:

> If time is mind-dependent, then reality (*real* – that is, mind-independent – reality) is altogether static and changeless. And then reality could provide no explanatory basis for *the change of mental states* experienced by all conscious organisms.

This objection rests on a basic error in reasoning from the premiss that the extra-mentally 'real' situation lacks (full-blooded) time, to the conclusion that it is unchanging and static. The appropriate alternative called for here is not changelessness but timelessness in the sense of the *atemporal*, that is, a situation in which the conception of time (in its full-blooded mode) is altogether inapplic-

---

[6] Note that at this stage of the argument it is important that what Russell called an *egocentric* particular (here/there, I/you, now/then) is involved: the crucial fact is that *an experience-defined particular* is at issue.

able. It is thus wholly misleading to think in terms of a basic (extra-mental) situation that is itself static but somehow dynamicized by mind. As we insisted above, one appropriate contrast with time is not the static and unchanging, but rather 'temporality' in a more restricted but yet change-admitting sense. The objection's complaints about the picture of a mentalistic emergence of time out of an utterly changeless ground is thus quite inappropriate. Change, process, and activity are indeed needed for our view of the mentalistic origin of (full-blooded) time, but our view of the (strictly speaking) literally *timeless* extra-mentalistic situation is not such that these are altogether unavailable.

Of course someone could still complain: 'How could the mind possibly generate A-series nowness out of mere B-series contemporaneity – as it would have to do on the view that time (*proper*, full-blooded time) is mind-dependent?' We could attempt to answer by a long discourse about the emergence of consciousness and the now-generative function of conscious awareness of contemporaneous co-presence. But all this can be short-circuited with the remark that the Western intellectual tradition has long ago abandoned the Greek principle of causality that only like can generate like. For us, unlike the Greeks, there is no intellectual difficulty about accepting the prospect that unlike should produce like or like unlike. This observation itself suffices to remove all its sting from the purported difficulty of locating the causal origin of the *now* in a ground of now-lacking temporality. The nowness of the present is, on our view, an inherently mentalistic factor, one which requires the perspective of an apprehending intelligence, and accordingly makes nowness a causal product of the workings of conscious awareness.

Another closely related objection to the thesis that time is mind-dependent goes as follows:

The view that time (full-blooded time) is somehow manufactured by minds and projected by them upon a time-less and so basically *static* situation is at bottom incoherent. For it calls upon minds to *do* something: it requires them to *act* and to change their activities. But how can there possibly be any change in mental activity and product if time itself is *created*

K

by minds. It is incongruous to the point of inconsistency to use a *productive* model for the origin of a dynamic time from a static causal ground.

The point of this objection is to claim an incongruity in conjoining a productionistic and activistic view of mind with the thesis that time is itself a product of the intervention of mind, so that the extra-mentalistic situation is timeless and therefore – it is said – static.

The materials for a reply to this objection are already in hand. Action, productivity, and change in general require no more than that B-series prototemporality whose mind-dependency we have already conceded. Thus to see the causal ground of time proper in a *static* condition is quite incorrect: a stopping short of capital-T Time just does not force one into a realm that is static and unchanging. Timelessness thus does not spell changeless constancy, and accordingly the inference of 'timeless and so static' commits a fallacy in not distinguishing between the temporal but constant and the altogether atemporal.

## 6. THE MIND-DEPENDENCY OF TIME NOT PSYCHOLOGICAL

The thesis that time is mind-dependent is sometimes met with the following objection:[7]

> If time is the product of mind, then is it not a miracle approaching the preestablished harmony of Leibniz that you and I and all of us produce the *same* time in which a common history weaves a uniform and orderly pattern of occurrences? If people somehow create time in their minds, how can it possibly be accounted for that everyone's time is properly coordinated.

Let us dub this problem as that of interpersonal coordination. In the framework of the present discussion its solution may be given along something like the following lines.

The mind-dependency envisaged in our theory is *not a matter of individual minds and personal psychology*; the issue just is not one of the idiosyncratic mental processes of particular conscious-

[7] Cp. F. Ferré, *op. cit.*

ness. In asserting the dependency of time (or other factors) upon minds, we have in view not *individual* minds but minds-in-general. The conceptual considerations we adduce do not point to a mind-dependency cast in the mold of *individual* psychology, but rather relate to generic mentalistic capacities shared by people in general. Any talk of full-blooded time with its inherent reference to the now-of-the-present-moment views a public and social situation. On this approach, when something is conceptualized as occurring 'now' this is not something experiential in any manner that is individualistic or idiosyncratic: rather, as its ostensive character as a *this* (this-moment) suggests, the 'now of the present' represents a fundamentally *public* conception against the background of a collective (social) situation in which interaction and communication are essentially operative. Time is not just a mentalesque but also a *social* construct.

There is nothing idiosyncratic about capital-T Time. As its involvement with measurability suggests, the very content of the conception of time proper is that of an interpersonal, public, objective, framework. Full blooded time requires (as we have argued) an inherent reference to presentness, and so to experience. But there must be room for the sharing of *common* experience in any social setting in which communication is to be possible. And this social framework of shared experience and a shared mechanism of communication endows the conception of time (i.e., the 'public time' of communicating mankind rather than the 'private time' of the psychologically idiosyncratic mind-life of the individual) with an impersonal aspect that frees it from all taint of subjectivity.

If time were the product of individual psychology as with the temporality of our dreams – if it were idiosyncratically disjoint from person to person – then interpersonal coordination would indeed be a miracle akin to the divinely inaugurated Pre-Established Harmony of Leibniz. But in fact time is not a construct of the psychology of the individual but rather a function of the shared (albeit mentalistically laden) communicative machinery of a social order. Accordingly, the problem of interpersonal co-ordination as to the time is solved *automatically* – or rather, does not arise as a genuine problem.

One could, of course, attempt to push the problem back to the metaphysical level and ask 'What is there about nature that makes possible the interpersonal constitution of a common time-order?' But this question fails, I think – at least in the first analysis – to pose a genuine difficulty. For if I had 'experiences' outside the common temporal order, ones that could not be inserted into temporal framework that we all share in common, we would *for this very reason* class them as delusive or illusory or hallucinatory, and deny them any status of cognitive meaningfulness. The reason why all our *experiences* of the real fit into a common time-framework is simply that we would automatically reject as unreal pseudo-experiences those that do not. The time-order of the real is as much a function of our concept of reality as of our concept of time.

## PART II: SPACE

### 7. THE MIND-DEPENDENCY OF SPACE

The line of reasoning to be followed in arguing here for the mind-dependency of space is fundamentally akin to that adopted with respect to time. Accordingly we are in a position to be quite brief.

It is profitable to adopt with respect to space a distinction – comparable to that previously drawn with respect to time – between *minimal spatiality* and *full-blooded space*. Basic spatiality calls for two factors:

(1) a plurality of *positions* which
(2) are placed relative to one within a certain characteristic *structure of ordering*.

These factors of *positionality* and *ordinality* are the starting-point from which a full-scale concept of space is developed by the addition of the two further factors of *orientation* and *distance-mensuration*.

(3) *orientation* represents the factor of *observer-relative* placement that giving rise to the applicability of the concepts of

'here' and 'there' that facilitate what might be characterized as spatial interiorization. Specifically, the idea of
'thereness' is so articulated everything positioned in space
is somehow *reachable from here by* 'tracking,' i.e., is *connected* with 'here' in a way underwritten by the conception of the *transport* of a continuously self-identical
particular. (It just is not a part of real space if one cannot
[in principle, at any rate] get there from here.) Space is
thus not simply a family of abstract *positions* but a framework for the location of *particulars*.

(4) Distance-*mensuration* represents the fact that for every
pair of positions in space it is in principle possible to determine by *measurement* a (unique and duly well-behaved)
numerical quantity, the *distance* between these positions.

The status of these four spatial factors is fundamentally analogous to that of their temporal cognates. Thus, positionality and
ordinality are both conceptually mind-invoking because a structure of *particular* (identified or identifiable) positions is at issue.
And clearly the specification of particular positions must proceed
through that of the 'spatial particulars' by reference to which
these positions can be differentiated. Furthermore, distance-mensuration also proves to be conceptually mind-invoking because
mensuration of all sorts – that of spatial distance specifically included – calls for the identification and reidentification of concrete
particulars, viz., the measuring instruments themselves. Moreover,
the behavior of these instruments in the context of their environment must be *lawful* in critical respects if *measurement* in any
meaningful sense is to result. Both of these points were treated
at some length in the discussion of time, and we need not repeat
ourselves here. Thus on both of two counts, that of particularity-
presupposition and that of lawfulness, the measurement of distance is mind-invoking.

Moreover, *spatial* measurement is specifically (unlike, e.g.,
chronometry or calorimetry) and by its nature an *iteratively
observational* procedure, one carried out by sequential steps in
such a way as to require 'noting the result' of every stage of the
process before going on with the rest. The very concept of spatial

distance is that of a procedure answering to multi-step instructions for the sequential use of an instrument such as a yardstick. A fundamentally *cognitive* process is involved. This aspect renders spatial measurement specifically as mind-invoking from yet another perspective.

There now remains the fourth, certainly crucial issue of spatial orientability. This factor of orientation introduces the element of outright mind-dependency. This is clear from its essential invocation of an observer-relative placement through the egocentric localization inherent in the here/there distinction, which is patently dependent upon its implementation upon the experiential awareness of conscious observers (just as is the case with the now-of-the-present-moment).[8]

The upshot of these considerations is thus essentially analogous to that arrived at in the preceding analysis of time. While there is indeed a minimal concept of a rudimentary or *proto*-spatiality, our full-blooded concept of space involves explicitly mind-dependent components.

But there still remains the objection which Ayer has formulated as follows: 'if space and time are merely forms of human sensibility, it follows that the Universe is co-terminous with the existence of the human race.'[9] This objection hits wide of the mark. Because spatiotemporal conceptions are applicable only from within the framework of a certain mind-involving perspective, this does not mean that if we *abrogate* this perspective, then these conceptions still *continue to apply and do so in such a way as to establish a limit*. To recognize spatiotemporality as a part of the intellectual contrivances of man does not mean that if there were no men then those aspects of the world in virtue of which these contrivances are applicable to it would be annihilated or altered. The division of a homogeneous sphere into parts is (presumably) wholly mind-dependent, but this does not mean that if there were no minds the sphere would collapse into

---

[8] To say this is not to deny that there may be crucial disanalogies between 'now' and 'here' but just to insist that each in *some* way relies upon the experience of conscious observers for its identification. (No doubt the specific circumstances of the two cases are quite different.)

[9] A. J. Ayer, *Metaphysics and Common Sense* (London, 1969), p. 65.

a point 'because then it would have no parts.' From the per-spective of the present considerations the crucial point is that of a conceptual mind-involvement: there is no question of any *causal* efficacy to produce changes in the world.

## 8. QUANTITY AND MEASUREMENT

It is necessary to block certain erroneous inferences that might possibly be drawn from this discussion. With regard both to time and space we have argued that measurability is a source of mind-involvement. The reader may be tempted to conclude that this represents a commitment to the view that *all quantitative aspects* of things are mind-involving. This is not so. There is on our view nothing mind-involving about quantitativeness *per se*.

To see how this is so, let us survey once more the specifically mind-invoking aspects of measurement:

(1) The very concept of measurement is inherently observa-tion-oriented; the process of a measurement being so conceived as to require the *noting* or *remarking* of certain particular results (viz., the 'outcome' of the several 'steps of the process'). Measurement is by nature an *experience-relative* procedure.

(2) The process of measurement requires the identification and reidentification of particulars (clocks, yardsticks, volt-meters, thermometers, etc.). Thus the argument that parti-cularity is mind-dependent affects measurement as well.

(3) The process of measurement is operative only in the con-text of laws governing the conditions and circumstances of the measuring process (the behavior of clocks, rods, etc.). Thus the argument that lawfulness is mind-dependent affects measurement as well.

Finally, and most crucially, measurement is a fundamentally cognitive process that invariably relates to a *discernible aspect of a particular* (the length of an interval, the duration of an episode, the humidity of a room, the price of a tract of land, etc.). The result of a measurement is always orientated towards the observa-tional features of particulars. One cannot just measure, one must measure *something* – measurement must relate to some empirical aspect of an identified item. And consequently the argument that the empirical features of particulars are mind-dependent leads to the consequence that measurement is of a like status.

Measurement relates to the empirical determination (through suitably contrived *observation*) of specifically quantitative aspects *of particular individuated things.* If we here abstract from the particularizing aspects of observation and individuation we are left simply with the generic idea of a quantitative dimension of 'things-in-general.' At this thing-abstractive and duly generic level, quantizability may well characterize 'objective reality' in its mind-independent aspect. Nothing we have said gainsays this prospect of a 'purely objective' quantification without particularity. That (unindividuated) 'things-in-general' have certain quantitative features in a manner that is nowise mind-invoking is not ruled out by the considerations we have adduced. But once we proceed to specify this quantification in terms of measurement (with its resort to particularity, observation, and laws) then – as our argument has it – we enter the domain of the conceptually mind-involving.

# Chapter VIII

# THE MIND-INVOLVEMENT OF THE PROPERTIES OF REAL PARTICULARS

## 1. GROUNDWORK

One describes the things that exist in nature – the furniture of this world – by indicating their qualities, features, and characteristics, and in particular by specifying their kind or type, that is, by classifying them in the rubric-schematism of some descriptively informative typology. The elements of all such various characterizations – of whatever mode they be – may for convenience be designated in common as *properties*.

It was argued in the preceding discussion that thinghood or *particularity* (i.e., *thing*-distinctness) is mind-involving. The present chapter seeks to argue – with various suitable qualifications and 'explanations' – the related thesis that *properties* (i.e., *type*-distinctions) are also conceptually mind-involving.

Our description of the specific particulars in the world is and must be cast primarily and preeminently in terms of their empirical properties. Even to specify a physical object (as *this X* – this deer or this apple), some reference to its *empirical* properties is needed – with this term taken in its root sense of experience and observation – because there could be no interpersonal identification without observational contact. (And, of course, going beyond mere *identification*, it is clear that the public and objective *description* of any specific natural particular will rely essentially and extensively upon a specification of its empirical properties.) The very idea of what is at issue envisages particulars as real or potential objects of experience, experience in which we obtain knowledge of objects through a knowledge of their properties. The manifest properties that we ascribe with fully objective *purport* to the things of our ordinary conceptual scheme are experiential and *observational*. It certainly will not do to hold that 'what we see – or otherwise experience – is without conceptual involvements.' For any such view shipwrecks on Kant's profoundly correct contention that percepts without concepts are blind. The specific mechanisms of our conceptual frameworks inform the products of our perception and conception of the particulars of nature. Throughout this domain, any rigid distinction between mental 'form' and material 'content' is altogether unworkable, because the formal elements inherent in our conceptual frameworks are decisively content-conditioning. Conceptualization, then, is an inescapable feature of all dealings with the particular objects of experiential encounter.

It is crucial at the very outset to distinguish between two possible versions of the thesis that properties are mind-involving, to wit

(1)  the *essentially factual* thesis of categorial – that is, category-bound – restrictedness, holding that those particular properties (quality-sortings and classifications) that figure centrally in the conceptual scheme or schemes that we *in fact* standardly employ in describing what exists in the world are all mind-involving.

and by contrast:

(2)  the *transcendental* thesis holding unrestrictedly that, on purely theoretical grounds of 'general principles,' any and all such properties must in principle and *of necessity* – in the conceptual nature of things – be somehow mind-involving.

With the former thesis regarding the mind-relatedness of natural properties, the stipulation of mind-involvement rests the issue basically on a matter of operative fact, as it were, while with the latter thesis it becomes one of theoretical principle. The present chapter is concerned only to argue for the first thesis, *not* the second. The crucial point for the position maintained here is simply that those properties which *de facto* comprise the framework of the standard conceptual scheme are in fact such as to be mind-invoking. We have no need to contend for the far more ambitious and dubious thesis that any and every conceptual scheme that might be devised as a vehicle for thought about 'the real world' is inevitably committed to being comparably mind-involving.

Thus no attempt is made here to present a *transcendental* argument that gets behind every possible conceptual scheme to argue that all properties must as such be inevitably mind-involving. We only maintain: (1) that those properties that relate to the central features of our standard conceptual scheme for thinking about the things in nature (space, time, causality, etc.) are mind-involving, and (2) that all *empirical* properties that represent experientially manifest features of things (color, form, etc.) are thereby mind-involving. Our 'deduction' of the mind-involvingness of the categories in terms of which we think of the real is not absolute and transcendental, but relative and factual: it does not rest on matters of *a priori* principle relating to the inevitable aspect of all humanly usable intellectual frameworks, but is framework-relative with respect to the inherent features a given conceptual scheme (namely the one we have characterized as 'our standard framework for conceptualizing the furniture of this world'). Acordingly, the present discussion will not argue generally and transcendentally that *any and all* recourse to properties involves an in-principle mind-invoking commitment. Rather, the more modest thesis is maintained that the mind-involvement at issue affects the key types of properties within the categorial scheme of descriptive characterization *which we in fact make use of* to characterize the furnishings of natural reality, one that places its prime stress on the *empirical* (i.e., observationally determinable) properties of things. The substantiation of this limited thesis is the primary task here.

## 2. EMPIRICAL PROPERTIES AS MIND-DEPENDENT

The mind-involvement of *dispositional* properties as inherently lawful suffices also to establish at once that of *all of our standard groupings of classification with respect to the lawful behavior of things*. And this has vast repercussions as regards the groupings of the classificatory system we standardly employ in our thought about nature. Thus the ascription to particulars of such classificatory features as 'being made of iron,' 'being made of glass' or of 'being a lion' or 'being a maple' is just as dispositional (and hence mind-invoking) as being malleable, or fragile or being a conductor.[1] The mind-involvement of dispositions is the 'thin end of the wedge' that can be used to establish the comparable status of all the empirical properties of the things of our ordinary, conceptual scheme that represent classifications linked essentially to lawful behavior.

This consideration of the mind-involvement of dispositional properties in general provides the starting point essential for present purposes. Indeed this fact provides the essential premiss for the key point that: *All empirical properties are mind-invoking.*

By an '*empirical* property' we shall here understand – quite in the literal sense of this term – one whose ascription to something reports the result of experiential contact (be it direct or indirect) with this item. Such properties by their very nature indicate how experiencing agents – or the instrumentalities they employ – normally or standardly react to or interact with the thing to which the property is ascribed in observation and analogous processes. A manifest color predicate like 'red' affords a paradigm example, because quite clearly any predicate that states how a thing standardly looks (or feels, smells, etc.) is patently mind-referential. But not only these 'predicates of sense-observation,' as we may call them, but those of any mode of 'observation' whatsoever – however complex the procedures and instrumentalities involved may be – are of this sort. All such predicates that embody a claim as to how something is standardly-observed-to-be are clearly mind-referential, because of the inherently mind-referential nature of observation *per se.* Observation, after all, is in its essential nature a process of interaction in which a mind is necessarily one of the items involved: it is inherent in the very concept that 'observing' is an *interaction* between a mind and some sector of reality. Thus even apart from the fact that complex modes of observations are (like measurement, as we have seen) dispositional and law-correlative – and so mind-involving – they are *also* mind-invoking because by their very nature they report the results of experiential interaction.

Our point can be made by means of a simple sorites:

The empirical properties of things are experiential

---

[1] Cf. K. R. Popper, *Conjectures and Refutations* (London, 1962), p. 387.

All experiential properties of things represent relational matters pertaining to their effects upon a perceiver

All properties pertaining to effects represent dispositional features of things[2]

All dispositional properties are law-involving

All law-involving features are mind-invoking

∴ The empirical properties of things are mind-invoking.

According to the position here in view, it is contended:

(1) Not that *all* properties are universally and necessarily mind-invoking, but only

(2) That *empirical* properties, the key properties we standardly use for the individuation and description of particulars, are mind-invoking.

Thus emphasis upon the empirical properties that are accesssible to us through observation and its instrument-supplemented congeners is central to the argument.

It is important to distinguish these *empirical* predicates of things, pertaining to their usual or standard, interpersonally and publicly accessible impact upon observers, with the *phenomenological* predicates of seeming and appearance. Consider the contrast between

(1) *is red* (in an objective, public way)

(2) *appears-to-be-red* (i.e., is red-looking, now, to me)

The former represents a stable and objective characterization that is essentially dispositional and for this reason mind-invoking since the disposition is mind-orientated. The phenomenological case is different but easier. That phenomenal properties that specify how things 'appear' (seem, are taken, etc.) – are mind-invoking goes practically without saying.

In sum, the observationally determinable empirical properties of things are mind-involving in a double way:

(i) they are essentially *dispositional*, ascribing features to

---

[2] On the essentially dispositional aspect of all manifest predicates see Nelson Goodman, *Fact, Fiction, and Forecast* (2nd ed., Indianapolis, 1965), pp. 40–49.

things in essentially law-correlative terms (and lawfulness is mind-involving).

(ii) and this disposition is itself mind-invoking because the impact at issue is by nature one that is made upon an experiencing mind (and so involves an inherent reference to mind).

Moreover, it is important to distinguish between empirical and theoretical properties. For empirical (*observational* and *phenomenological*) properties contrast also with the theoretical (i.e., theory-based) properties familiar from the sciences. (Consider, for example, the contrast between 'is a conductor' [said of a piece of metal] on the one hand and 'is shiny' or 'is yellowish' on the other.) The foregoing discussion has concentrated upon the experientially manifest properties of things. But what of theoretical properties? There may perhaps be some non-standard cases here, but in the standard case, a theoretical property is one attributed to something on the basis not of observation as such, but as part of a theoretical account for aspects of the functioning of the thing (like the magnetism of a magnet). But all *such* properties are dispositional, and thus law-correlative, and consequently mind-involving (in accordance with the preceding argument that dispositionality and lawfulness in general represent mind-invoking conceptions). And so, while theoretical descriptive terms may, admittedly, fail to be directly observational (and so not mind-invoking in the dispositional manner at issue above), they are still inherently dispositional: since scientific predicates are inevitably applied only to characterize some *interactional* aspect of things.[3] And this too introduces the critical factor of mind-involvement.

[3] Note that with *people* we might well draw a distinction between those properties they have 'in themselves' (e.g., being intelligent or Spanish or music-loving) and those properties that indicate the impact they make upon others (e.g., being confident-inspiring, repulsive, amusing, likeable, or the like). This clearly carries over into our talk about things (e.g., a statue can be bronze and Venus-representing on the one hand and lifelike and striking upon the other). Now the point is that those scientific predicates that are not essentially classificatory (*felix leo*) or stuff-indicative (carbon, gold) are – virtually – all of the impact-on-other things-indicative types (conductor, acid, predator, etc).

The upshot of this analysis may thus be summarized in the thesis of the fundamental and indeed double mind-invokingness of the empirical properties of things – be they observational or theoretical – as dispositions standardly to produce (directly or indirectly) certain characteristic results, results that are themselves of a mind-referring nature.

The following objection to the present thesis may be made. 'You have granted that things can have objective (mind-independent) properties. But when the empirical, and so according to you mind-involving property $\phi$ is attributed to some item, then it must surely bear some objective (mind-independent) feature $\phi'$ in virtue of which this attribution is appropriate and correct. And it is this objective $\phi$-counterpart $\phi'$ – the objective ground of the item's $\phi$-hood – that really is ultimately at issue.' We answer this objection by rejecting one of its essential premisses, the thesis that

When $\phi$ is (correctly) attributable to something, then it must have some objective feature $\phi'$ in virtue of which this attribution is correct.

We reject this because we maintain that the feature 'in virtue of which' the item has an empirical property $\phi$ is not a proper (absolute) property of it at all, but a *relational* property in which its relationship to the observer is crucially operative. It is through this mind-pertaining *relational* aspect of the grounds for $\phi$ that mind-dependence arises in such a way as to preclude 'objectivity' (in the mind-excluding sense at issue in the objection). This relational aspect of features and their grounds needs further explanation.

Let us recall the discussion of lawfulness in Chapters IV and V. This led to the result that all properties that are *dispositional* in nature – that is, properties which deal, like *malleability* or *solubility*, with the behavior of things 'in certain circumstances' and thus bear an essentially hypothetical burden of what-would-happen-if – are mind-invoking because of their tacit reference to unrealized possibilities. It should be stressed that the hypothetical element at issue here extends well beyond the sphere of overt and explicit laws, to encompass all dispositional predicates such as 'malleable,' 'soluble,' 'fragile,' etc., as well as cognate dispositionally classificatory nouns such as 'conductor' (of electricity), 'catalyst' (in certain chemical processes), etc., which also have an intrinsically hypothetical element. The cube of sugar is *soluble* in that '*if* it is immersed in water for a sufficient period, *then* . . .'; the copper wire is a conductor because '*if* an electric charge is placed at one extreme, *then* . . .' Applications of all such dispositional nouns and predicates are implicitly lawful. Thus our analysis of the mind-involving implications of lawfulness is operative here also.

### 3. AN OBJECTION

It is an immediate implication of the line of thought just presented that 'being *identified*' is fundamentally different from 'being *classified*' in terms of a property-specification. The identificatory discrimination of distinct items is, as we have maintained, an inherently mind-involving process that in principle cannot just reflect the mind-independent fact of an 'objective identity.' But there is – so we now maintain – no comparable reason of fundamental principle why a *descriptive assimilation* of things cannot rest on a foundation of strictly objective and mind-independent similarity.

Now this divergence in approach to thing-identification and type-classification opens the way for the following seemingly weighty objection:

How can you consistently admit the prospect that property-ascription may conceivably rest on a mind-independent basis of an objective similarity among things when you have already argued that thinghood itself is mind-dependent? How can the similarity of item *A* and item *B* be strictly objective (in the sense of being altogether mind-independent), if these items *themselves* are mind-dependent? How could things be 'objectively alike' if these very things are themselves constituted as such mind-dependently?

The objection is – in its own way – well taken. If 'things' are themselves regarded as being mind-constituted *as such*, then one can hardly maintain that *their* similarity in point of properties is wholly independent of mind. But the present position is not forced into this anomaly.

For one thing, we need not in principle view the 'objective' similarity in question as a similarity between individuated *things* at all. Not *item*-similarity but *stuff*-similarity can be at issue – i.e., not the similarity of this air bubble to that air bubble or this nail to that nail, but of air to air or iron to iron. The distinction between composition-indicative mass-nouns (water, iron, wood) and sort-indicative count-nouns (glasses of water, pieces of iron) – the former representing *stuff* and the latter *items* – is sufficiently familiar that we need not belabor it. With stuff rather than items – wine and water for example – we can have similarity without any discrete *things* entering upon the stage at all. The case is, of course, wholly altered when we consider 'made of iron' in the status of a predicate of an *individuated* something (e.g., this nail). To consider types of stuff under the aspect of generality is quite different from considering specific instances or pieces or chunks of stuff under the aspect of particularity. Universals as particular-pertaining *item-collecting* principles of plurality-into-unity are mind-involving because individuated *items* are. But universals as generic *stuff-unifying* principles of unity-into-plurality are not necessarily mind-involving. In short, since properties need not represent the features of particular *individuated* things, there is nothing inconsistent in granting the possible objectivity (non-mind-involvement) of *properties* in the face of an insistence upon the mind-invocation of *things*.

However, this particular way out of the difficulty, though perhaps available in some abstractly theoretical way, is not in practice open to us because of the argument given above to the effect that the manifest types of stuff of our ordinary conceptual scheme (water, iron, wood, etc.), being correlative with distinctions based upon lawful behavior, will themselves be mind-invoking on this ground.

A second way out of the preceding difficulty must thus be found. Fortunately one is available. For one can maintain that individuated things are, as such, mind-invoking, and *then* go on to argue that once things so mind-involvingly constituted are at

L

hand, no *further* mind-invoking aspect is needed for properties to obtain. Antecedent and consequent mind-invocation should accordingly be distinguished. If individuated things are mind-invoking then *everything about THEM* is mind-invoking antecedent to their constitution. But *once constituted*, their further aspects need not involve any *additional* mind-invocation. Thus, *in this consequent sense*, there may be objective and essentially mind-independent similarities between things that as such (i.e., as the discriminated things they are) are themselves mind-involving. An analogy is useful here: the meaning of words is conventional and arbitrary, but no *further* arbitrariness need affect the statements we make by their means.[4]

### 4. POSTSCRIPT

The preceding discussion has left quite open the prospect that there might be properties of the furnishings of the natural world -- conceived not as a plurality of *individuated things* but one of different *kinds of stuff* -- that are not mind-involving. But such properties have to be of a very peculiar sort. For these mind-independent properties cannot be empirical, nor of course, phenomenological, nor of the *standardly* theoretical sort (i.e., dispositional), since all these are mind-involving. They would have to be *nonstandardly* theoretical -- because they will have to be entirely nonobservational properties of a strictly non-dispositional kind. These would, of course, be something rather odd, but *odd* does not mean *impossible*. Our position thus departs from that sector of idealist tradition -- beginning with the 'Parmenidist' view considered in Plato's *Parmenides* with its prospect that the *forms* may be *thoughts* -- that regards *all* property-ascription as such to be inevitably mind-dependent.

Striking consequences follow when once it is recognized that all of the properties of things we can possibly know in experience are

----

[4] The case is analogous to the distinction between absolute and hypothetical necessity. That today is Tuesday is not necessary as such and antecedently. But *given* that yesterday was Monday, it is, *consequent* to this datum, utterly necessary: no *further* data are requisite to its demonstrative establishment.

dispositionally relational in representing dispositions to produce certain effects upon perceivers or their instrumental surrogates. For one thing, it follows that we can have no experiential (and so noninferential) knowledge of the absolute (= nondispositional) properties of things. And since all empirically dispositional properties are (doubly) mind-invoking, it follows that all of the properties of things that we know in experience are mind-involving.

The present position is essentially Leibnizian. With Leibniz, it holds that the *manifest* (i.e., observational) properties of the things-of-common-experience – the spatial and the temporal properties included – are all 'phenomenal' (in the Leibnizian sense of being in some way mind-dependent); whereas those properties – whatever they be – that metaphysically ultimate things 'in themselves' may really and objectively and mind-independently have, are wholly nonobservational and so – from our angle – of an altogether theoretical nature. (For Leibniz they are purely intelligible, and so accessible to God alone, though clearly not by an *observational* process.)

This position, of course, touches only the sphere of concrete, experientiable objects – i.e., those we can actually encounter in the observational realm. It does not touch the domain of objects conceived of as purely theoretical constructs, such as the atoms of Democritus, the aether of classical physics, or the antimatter of contemporary particle theory. But, of course, to conceive of something in these terms as a *theoretical* entity is to ascribe a mind-involving status to it in our conceptual sense. To be sure, it need not be something mentalistic in character, but is such that mental capabilities need to be brought in to give a full and adequate account of the thing at issue. And clearly, something whose very condition of being (its 'ontological status') is said to be theoretical is obviously being conceived of in mind-invoking terms. Moreover – and this is the crucial point – the reason for being of a theoretical entity is to serve as the bearer of theoretical properties, and these are standardly mind-invoking in line with the preceding dispositional analysis.

On such a view, there is nothing in the conception of actuality as such that renders it as somehow mind-involving in abstract principle.⁵ No such transcendental conclusion lies within the range of present considerations. We have merely argued that the situation *in practice* is in this regard quite different, since the actuality of our *standard* conceptual scheme is in crucial respects mind-involving. The descriptive concepts through which we in fact conceptualize actuality are all heavily invested with undercurrents of lawful and possibilistic reference – specifically to dispositions, capabilities, capacities, powers, processes, and the like. And this feature of covert possibilistic reference to our standard actuality-characterizing concepts renders them (tacitly) mind-invoking in the final analysis. Accordingly, what is on this view mind-involving in regard to actuality is not actuality *per se*, but *our* actuality – that is, reality according to our standard ways of thinking of it (as a collection of discrete things with observationally determinable properties, located in space and time, interacting causally, etc.). The burden of the conceptual idealism we have articulated is that, by thinking of the real in terms that coordinate it with fundamentally *possibilistic* concepts, we conceive of it in inherently mind-referring terms.

⁵ Chapter II above has already given a substantial discussion of the differences in this regard between actuality and possibility.

# Chapter IX

# AN IDEALIST THEORY OF NATURE

## 1. STAGESETTING

Those aspects of our conceptual idealism that relate to the philosophy of nature deserve closer scrutiny. But first a brief review is in order. The discussion has throughout been oriented towards the 'standard conception' of nature as an aggregation of physical particulars emplaced in space and time and interacting causally. Our conceptual idealism has been articulated through an analytical unraveling of the key concepts operative in this view of nature, an unraveling that has sought to bring their mind-invoking aspects to light. Possibility was held to be mind-involving because of its essential involvement with mental processes of conceiving, supposing, hypothesizing and the like. Causality involves lawfulness which in turn is to be understood in terms of possibility. The individuation of particulars is mind-involving in its actualistic aspect because it is conceptually linked to identification (an inherently mentalistic process), and in its possibilistic aspect both for this very reason of possibility-invocation and because laws are involved. Finally, space and time are both to be understood through a reference to individuals and to laws, and are in consequence also mind-involving for the aforesaid reasons.

Accordingly, the critical aspect of mind-invocation affects our conceptualization of physical particulars from various directions:

(1) in being conceived of as particulars, and so possessed of a discrete and separate individuality.

(2) in being individuated through empirical properties and descriptive sortals and so receiving classificatory placement in a law-involving taxonomic scheme.

(3) in being conceived of as placed within the ordering frameworks of space and time (of the full-blooded variety) and causality.

The key fact is that the realm of things that comprise nature-as-we-standardly-think-of-it is conceptualized by us in terms of reference that reflect their own mentalistic origin.

The implications of these considerations for our view of the nature of reality must be scrutinized in detail. Let us begin by considering the prospect of a world described in terms purified of all noomorphic mind-invoking conceptions, the sort of 'purely objective' *residue* of *an sich* reality that remains when all mind-invoking concepts are erased from our standard view of the world – the terminus of a total denuding of its mind-involving facets.

The *terra incognita* to be reached along this route is not a very profitable realm of exploration. A world conceived along strictly mind-independent lines could not, from *our* point of view, seem very interesting. For how would a natural world have to be conceived of if this were to be done without any trace of mind-involvement?

Such a world-concept would have the following features:

(1) It would be a world without particularity. A world of generic stuff and not specific things.

(2) There might well be a plurality of stuff-kinds, but they would not fall into empirically determinate or determinable varieties. From our conceptual perspective the world would be a chaos because its various stuff-kind components would not be empirically discriminable.

(3) The world might be protospatial and prototemporal, but would lack a properly spatio-temporal order. (Still, though full-scale space and time are lacking, there still remains room for variegation and change at the generic level.)

(4) It would be an *amodal* world – a realm without any aspects of modal differentiation. Whatever is, is so in a Humean way, *de facto* and without any coloration of necessity and possibility.

(5) It would be a world in which there might be abstract patterns of regularity but no causal order; an anomic world – one without laws, and without causal interaction or *process* in the accepted sense of this term. (In such a

world it makes no sense to ask 'what would happen if . . . ?')

(6) It would be a world that lacks the entire potentialistic domain of powers, capacities, dispositions, and the like.

We thus travel the *via negativa* of mind-independency to a rather bleak destination: not, to be sure, altogether the near-total emptiness and vacuity of the Kantian *Ding an sich*, but something rather close to it. And in any case, what we reach along this route is something radically *discontinuous* with our standard conception of the world.

## 2. A CRITIQUE OF COUNTERPART REALISM

The nature of this discontinuity deserves closer scrutiny. The untenability of what might be called *counterpart-realism* comes to light through the invalidity of the conception of 'metaphysically real counterparts' to the manifest objects of our everyday experience. Philosophers throughout history have been tempted to apply the distinction between appearance and reality to the objects of experience, contrasting (say) 'the tree as I perceive it over there' with 'the real tree as it is in itself.' From such a perspective, it seems natural to differentiate between on the one hand *the experientially manifest object* as we perceive it (having the ordinary sensuously apprehended properties of color, odor, shape, and the like) and, on the other, *the real object* corresponding to the former but having only such properties and features as are strictly mind-independent.

On one version of this doctrine of metaphysical realism, what is held to be real is not the-object-as-we-experience-it, but the *mind-independently real object* that is supposed to have only those properties and features that are altogether mind-independent. (This line of thought bears some analogy with Eddington's well-known distinction between the ordinary, familiar 'illusory' table of common sense and the physicists' 'real' table.[1] For over and above the manifest object of experiential familiarity – the

---

[1] Sir Arthur Eddington, *The Nature of the Physical World* (Cambridge and New York, 1928), pp. ix–x.

table as we know it – Eddington postulates something quite different: the physicists' table, 'the real physical object of the scientist.')

The idea of an Eddington-like 'metaphysically real counterpart' to the table breaks down, because if we proceed in altogether mind-independent terms we will be unable *in principle* to take cognizance of specific particulars, and so cannot deal with real particulars corresponding to those manifest in our standard view of the things of nature. The project of a *counterpart*-realism of mind-independently real objects as extra-mental versions of experienced particulars cannot be made to succeed. Such a supplementary realm of utterly mind-independent objects is uninhabitable, if only for the reason (already considered at length) that: all particularity requires the prospect of ostensive identification on the basis of experiential contact. If there are literally no mind-relative interactions upon the scene – not even 'in principle' and *in modo potentialitatis* – then there can be no identification and so no particularity. IF the metaphysician is to view the world from the conceptual perspective of a *purely mind-independent* orientation – and, of course, it is by no means essential that he do so – THEN he just will not obtain any counterpart table; indeed he will not obtain any particulars at all. There can be no correspondence between our familiar 'manifest' objects (tables, trees, etc.) on the one hand, and on the other the purportedly corresponding mind-independently real particulars, because one side of this correspondence fails us. The realm of altogether mind-independent *particulars* is simply vacuous. This form of scientific dualism must fail, because the conceptual schemes of manifest objects and of the 'mind-independently real' are drastically discontinuous.

The conception of an altogether mind-independent reality is not self-contradictory, but is an essentially empty idealization. It leads us along an ontological *via negativa* towards the *Ding an sich* of Kant and Bradley's Absolute. We arrive at no conceptually stable terminus but only at something of which we know that we can know nothing of it in terms of our conceptual scheme. It would be wholly in vain to attempt to distinguish between the table we see and the table as it *really* looks – as apart from this or that (restrictive) visual perspective: this very line of thought is quite unworkable. And exactly the same holds for the distinction between the chair as we conceive of it and the chair as it really is, wholly apart from this or that mind-invoking perspective. The idea of a concrete particular whose characterization is denuded of all mind-invoking conceptions is simply unworkable.

If we think in terms of a 'great divide' between on the one hand a sphere of the mind-involvingly real that is 'our reality,' and on the other an altogether mind-independent reality, then we will ultimately come to realize that the entire conceptual machinery for dealing with particulars through their identification (viz., space and time, causality, description) applies only on 'our' (mind-involving) side. To take the objectivistic approach at issue is to commit the sort of category mistake that results from confounding different and divergent conceptual schemes, by un-critically carrying the concept of particularity operative in our standard view of the world over into a region where it has no place: a 'world' in whose conceptualization there is to be no room for any element of mind-invocation. To say this is not to deny that the world 'really' is as we learn it to be in scientific or in philosophical theorizing, but rather to maintain that the world in view when one systematically avoids all mind-involving devices is genuinely disjoint from the 'manifest' world of everyday life.

### 3. CONCEPTUAL NOOMORPHISM

So far, then, we have the thesis that even the most basic elements of our view of nature are themselves mind-conditioned. This view, of course, is not *spiritualism* (the thesis that nature is made up of minds or 'mental stuff'). The way in which some-thing is mind-involving in the conceptual manner at issue here may be characterized as *noomorphic* – from the Greek *nous*. (It is not thereby necessarily *anthropomorphic*, since we need not be quite so parochial about the possession of minds.) That is, the fundamental components of our knowledge about reality are items in whose conceptual make-up there is operative an essential reference (however tacit or covert) to minds and their capabilities. Mind enters into any adequate account of our key concepts here – not perhaps directly and overtly, but as an ultimate presupposition. This *conceptual noomorphism* maintains the thesis that the concepts we standardly deploy in our thought about nature, and that we use to map out the world-as-we-conceive-of-it, are in part framed on the analogy of mind and formed by mind *in its own terms* by the use of essentially mind-involving conceptions.[2]

The case for this noomorphism can be sketched as follows: (1) Certain conceptual categories are central for our standard view of the world of nature and the nature of the world, to wit: the realm of particulars attuned to a descriptive framework of thing and property, space and time, and causality. (2) But all of these categories can upon due analysis be shown to be ultimately mind-invoking in diverse but fundamental respects. In all these critical respects, reality-as-we-think-of-it is a mental construct *in whose construction mentalesque elements play a substantial part.*

Is this noomorphic aspect of '*our* world' contingent or necessary as a feature of '*the* world?' It is certainly not necessary in any absolute sense; other conceptual schemes are certainly conceivable, schemes that dispense with the essential elements of the ordinary one – and thus doubtless appear grotesque from its standpoint. And moreover, it is certainly possible to think of the world in that very sparse and barren mind-abstracted way we have tried to indicate from time to time; so empty in content as to be reminiscent of the Kantian *an sich.* The point is just that IF we are to think of a (the) world *along the lines we in fact standardly employ* (i.e., in terms of particulars emplaced in space and time, falling into natural kinds, and interacting causally),

[2] Note once again that we have no need here to resort to the Absolute Spirit or Cosmic Mind or *Weltgeist* of absolute idealism: it is simply a matter of the claim that the mind conceives of the things of nature not only on its own terms but also at least in part in its own image, i.e., in terms of mentalistic processes and capabilities. The sort of mind-dependency at issue here is thus not subjective but roots in the generic, public, interpersonal capacities of minds.

THEN we must, as it were *ex hypothesi*, think of the world in mind-involving terms. The necessity of our noomorphism is in this sense not absolute but relative; relativized, that is, to the constitution of the ordinary conceptual scheme. (It is in this resort to an ultimately contingent basis in the *de facto* realities of our conceptual scheme that our conceptual idealism takes what is perhaps its most radical departure from the transcendental necessitarianism of Kant.)

On this idealist view, the mind not only makes its self-evidently essential contribution to our *knowing* 'the objects of experience' (that is, to the fact *that* we know them), but also to our *knowledge* of them (that is, to *what* we know of them), because we conceptualize the things of the world about us in terms that appear upon careful analysis as in part relativized to minds and their actions and capabilities. The intellectually ordered world of our experience is in part (but always in crucial part) shaped or constructed by mind in terms involving a reference to our capabilities. Not only does the mind contribute essentially to the conceptualizing *transaction* that is essential to experience, but certain key aspects of its contribution are made in effectively mentalistic terms. Key elements of the standard conceptual scheme being patterned on mind, we accordingly think of things, either overtly or covertly, in ways whose full explication requires mentalistic terms of reference, conceiving key aspects of reality in specifically mind-oriented ways.

In this regard, our idealism goes beyond a rationalistic insistence upon the contributory role of mind in the formulation (and indeed *formation*) of empirical information, by stipulating that at least a part of what the mind thus contributes is *always* in fact *formed in its own image*. Various key conceptual mechanisms deployed in the identification and description of empirical things are based upon a reflexive reference by the mind to its own functionings. The noomorphist theory maintains that our picture of reality is in essential part painted with the coloration of mind.

## 4. TRANSACTIONISM

The focus of the conceptualistic idealism presented in these pages is the idea that reality-as-we-conceive-it (within the conceptual framework we standardly employ in thinking about the world) is not merely conceived by minds, but conceived by them in terms that involve reference to their own workings and capabilities. On this view, the mind's articulation of our knowledge of things does not simply mirror in passive unmodified duplication the features that its objects objectively possess in an altogether mind-independent manner. Man's perception-based conception of the things-in-the-world is throughout *transactional*, with both the mind and extra-experiential nature conjointly making an individually indispensable and mutually inseparable contribution to the result. A sort of 'chemical' interaction takes place, so that no inference regarding the nature of the components can be warranted from any examination of the product. Such transactionism is a version of rationalism in holding that mind makes its (unfactorable and unisolable) contribution to our knowledge of nature. And accordingly it abandons the position of traditional realism that the cognitive subject is a 'pure spectator of independent reality' in that the objects of knowledge have a status altogether independent of the knower and his thought about them. Rather, the knower is viewed as a contributory *agent* in any situation of knowledge-productive encounter with 'the real world.'

A transactionist theory of the relation between 'independent reality' and 'perceived reality' must accept the consequences of the causal character of the relationship. Preeminently, it must face the fact that the gap from cause to effect can be crossed only by theory, and not by experience (Hume), nor by analogy, nor by invocation of the Greek axiom that like causes like. Causal inference from our experience towards its extra-experiential grounds demands a resort to inferred or theoretical entities. And since the properties of such entities must be altogether dispositional, we are constrained to think of the theory-indicated grounds of our experience in essentially mind-invoking terms.

(Thus the theory-accessible realm of the extra-experiential is by no means extra-mental in character if 'extra-mental' is to be construed as precluding the essential application of mind-involving conceptions.[3]) Accordingly, if things *an sich* are to be thought of as altogether freed of mind-involvement, then the *an sich* realm is not coextensive with but exclusive from that of the grounds of experience. (This position is simply a consequence of our view that since causality is mind-invoking, causal efficacy precludes the 'objectifying' removal of mind-involvement). We must accordingly not confuse the idea of a noumenal, extra-experiential *ground* of experience (a 'theoretical construct' which must, *qua* ground, be thought of in mind-invoking terms) and that of a near-vacuous *an sich* reality (as strictly objective and articulated in rational abstraction from any mode of mind-involvement).

The transactionalist is no skeptic regarding the realm of extra-experiential reality; his position is that a noumenal or extra-experiential reality exists, and that 'our world' of experienced reality is the product of a genuine *transaction* between it and the mind. Accordingly, while we cannot use *phenomenological* analysis to separate out the respective contributions made by mind and extra-experiential reality, we can, by the *scientific* analysis of phenomena, make at the level of generality certain generic claims regarding the constitution of this sector of 'objective reality' (claims which are theoretical in nature, and by no means free of mind-invocation in content).

It is, in effect, this transactionalist mode of idealism that we have espoused here, recognizing an extra-experiential reality that is not mind-independent, and combining this with a rather strong self-denying ordinance as to the rigid limits upon claims that can be made about the realm of strictly objective, *an sich* reality in altogether extra-mental terms. For if our standard view of reality is articulated in mind-invoking terms of reference

---

[3] We would thus do well to distinguish noumenal reality (= extra-experiential or extra-phenomenal reality) from reality *an sich* (= the extra-mental reality of the altogether mind-independent). For theory-based scientific information is, on our view, achievable with respect to the former, but *not* the latter. This distinction, though drawn in Kantian terminology, cannot be attributed to Kant as it stands here.

(as we have argued), then it is in principle impossible that it could somehow resemble or reproduce 'objective reality' if this is thought of as altogether mind-independent. Accordingly, one admits the fundamentally self-defeating nature of an attempt to say in mind-invoking terms what something (viz., strictly objective and altogether mind-independent 'reality') is mind-independently like.

Transactionism contrasts with an *assembly theory* of perceptual knowledge, cast in an essentially architectonic mold. An assembling approach would have it that materials are somehow delivered to it in finished units (like bricks to a construction site), and that the mind then assembles these units into structures (buildings). Such a theory is grossly misleading. There just are no mind-untouched experiential building-blocks which mind first receives and then assembles. Mind from the very outset touches and pervades everything experiential. In the perceptual knowledge of things one simply cannot separate out the mind-involving contributions to arrive at some residue, some mind-untouched 'remainder' characteristic of the *an sich* of things.

This view is essentially Kantian in spirit. For Kant, the fundamental question is: 'What can "pure reason" know of the things-of-the-world?' Here 'pure' carries the force of 'independently of the mind-imposed conditions of experience.' For reasons too complex to summarize here, Kant's answer comes simply to: nothing whatsoever. For us, the analogous question becomes: What can one know of the things-of-the-world in 'purely objective' terms, with 'purely objective' construed as 'independently of any and all use of mind-invoking conceptions?' And our answer is once again Kant's: nothing whatever. This is so, on our view, for the very fundamental reason that any talk – or thought – of *particular* things inevitably calls for their initial individuation, which is – as we have argued – possible only in mind-invoking terms. Accordingly, we join Kant in viewing any attempt to deal with natural particulars in totally mind-detached terms as doomed to an utter vacuity.

## 5. THE CONCEPT OF REALITY 'AN SICH'

The idealist position maintained here holds that the things of nature are standardly envisaged in terms of a conceptual machinery that is substantially imbued with mind-involving elements. Such an idealism seemingly invites the tempting prospect of imagining an *an sich* reality, a natural world conceived of in ways totally denuded of mind-involving concepts, and so strictly objective and mind-independent. But this conception of reality *an sich* needs closer scrutiny. In particular I want to explore the consequences that follow from the following two assumptions:

(1) *Particularity-Empiricism*: Our only cognitive access to the *particulars* of this world is in experience; experiential contact (*'thisness'*) alone provides the ultimate basis of evidence that is the foundation upon which all our knowledge of natural particulars must in the final analysis be based.

(2) *Transactionism:* All our experiential knowledge is a matter of a causal transaction between the extra-experiential ground of our experiencing and the mind that does the experiencing. The nature of this transaction is 'chemical' and permits no attribution of specific aspects to the separate elements of the transaction (mind, extra-experiential nature).

Our present concern is not with these premises themselves (which have already been argued for), but solely with the implicational question of the consequences that result from these two theses.

It deserves note that a whole sequence of significant implications of markedly Kantian flavor follow immediately from the fundamental asumptions of particularity-empiricism and transactionism:

(1) Our knowledge of particulars rests on a *causal* base; it is a product derived ultimately from the effects that the extra-experiential basis of our experiencing exerts upon us (through action on our sense-receptors, etc.).

(2) Our experiential knowledge (noninferential knowledge, knowledge by immediate acquaintance) of the properties

of particulars is altogether limited to certain of their *dispositional* properties, namely those representing their capacities to stimulate certain (presumably standard) reactions in us or in our observational surrogates. Such dispositional properties are fundamentally *relational*: they do not represent features of things as such, but rather pertain to the issue of how things are related to others.

(3) Our knowledge of the *proper* properties of particulars (that is, their *absolute* [= nonrelational] and *internal* [= nondispositional] properties) is accordingly restricted to *inferential* knowledge. All of their proper properties are thus *theoretical* properties: properties that do not present themselves in experience, as it were, but rather are ascribed on systematic (discursively theoretico-conjectural) grounds.

(4) Given that nothing whatever can be said of their proper properties outside a theoretical setting, since the only properties that can be claimed for them extra-theoretically are dispositional properties, these objects *themselves* are theoretical constructs ('inferred entities'). As far as experience goes, we do not know what they *are*, but only what they *do*.

(5) On a transactional/causal view of perception, the status of 'extra-experiential reality' is thus wholly theoretical. We can have no experiential information regarding the properly constitutive features of things, but only *impute* such features to particulars in the *theoretical* interests of explaining their experientially manifest features. We cannot cross the gulf between the dispositional properties presumably present in experience and the proper properties of things by any inferential process whatever, but only by an *imputation* built into the systematic framework of a theory.

(6) Accordingly, while there is a useful place for the conception of an extra-experiential, or extra-phenomenal, *noumenal* reality whose status is that of a theoretical construct, the case is otherwise as regards the conception of a reality *an sich* that is to be conceived of in altogether mind-independent terms of reference. For this last route takes us to a land too barren and infertile to be cognitively serviceable regarding 'the things of our world.'

In consequence, conceptual idealism stands perfectly prepared to accept a noumenal, experience-transcending reality accessible through theory alone. But it regards this not in Kant's way, as an ultimate postulate of objectivity, but rather as a mediate 'postulate of explanatory systematization.' Its role is *not* the Kantianly regulative one of furnishing a basis for the *objective validity* of our experience (lest we fall from a transcendental into a substantive idealism), by providing the relatum for the relation of appearing. The postulate is *not* needed to provide a causal ground of appearances (which is already inherent in the dispositional properties themselves); rather, it provides the mechanisms for a systematic rounding-out of our experience in the framework of a theory of nature.

In the interests of clarifying this position, it is useful to consider it from the perspective of some related but divergent lines of argument to the effect that knowledge of noumenal (= extraexperiential) objects is in principle impossible.

## A. *The Kantian Route*

The line of thought to be characterized as the Kantian Route to the conclusion that we have no knowledge of particulars 'in themselves' is encapsulated in the following argument:

(1) Knowledge regarding anything as it really is 'in itself' requires information regarding its proper (and so nondispositional) properties.

(2) Our knowledge of the properties of natural particulars is restricted to the products of direct (nondiscursive) experience.

(3) All experience and observation can in principle only provide information regarding the dispositional properties of extra-mental reality, never the absolute ones.

*Therefore* we have no knowledge of objects as they are 'in themselves.'

This line of thought may properly be characterized as Kantian because it is in spirit close to the master's line of thought. Kant, in separating reality from 'mere' appearance (or representation), held that the realm of natural things *as represented* 'contains nothing but mere relation' (B 66–7), and so does not possess objective reality.[4]

We ourselves, however, are not prepared to endorse this Kantian result. For we reject the second premiss of the argument. Even if one accepts the thesis that our knowledge of the properties of natural particulars must ultimately rest on or derive from the (nondiscursive) deliverances of experience – that experience lies, so to speak, at the center of this sector of the cognitive realm – this does not mean that the total domain of knowledge cannot transgress the boundaries of this narrow confine. We need not restrict authentic knowledge of objects to the information obtained in experience, if we are willing also to admit of theory-based knowledge, accessible through indirect (discursive rather than experiential) routes. Thus the collapse of its second premiss invalidates the argument as a path to its conclusion. The key factor here is the distinction between *noumenal* (= extra-phenomenal) reality, about which a great deal can be known in scientific theorizing, and *an sich* (= 'purely objective,' altogether mind-independent) reality, about which precious little can be known from the point of departure of the standard conceptual scheme we deploy in science and everyday life alike.

## B. *The Skeptical Route*

What may deservedly be characterized as the Skeptical Route of argumentation for agnosticism regarding the nature of particulars 'in themselves' follows the path of the argument:

1. Our information regarding the nondispositional aspects of the particular objects of our experience is altogether inferential (and, of course, nondeductively inferential).
2. Information derived by a nondeductively inferential process is never certain.

*Therefore*, we do not actually know anything about the nondispositional aspects of particulars – for knowledge must be certain – but we can only assume, hypothesize, or conjecture about them.

[4] Cf. also W. Sellars, *Science and Metaphysics* (London, 1968), p. 51 (§ 54), and pp. 54–5 (§ 66).

We once more reject the argument, being enabled to do so by our nonacceptance of the implications inherent in the implicit premiss that 'knowledge must be certain.' On our view, the force of the (perfectly acceptable) certainty-of-knowledge thesis is not such as to preclude the prospect of nondeductively inferential knowledge. to represent *knowledge*, information need not be 'certain' pure and simple, but merely as certain as, under the circumstances, it possibly could be.[5]

## C. *The Phenomenalist Route*

The Phenomenalist Route bars the prospect of knowledge regarding objects 'in themselves' (i.e., extra-experiential objects), because it denies their very existence. It proceeds by way of the argument:

1. Objects 'in themselves' are inferred entities (as maintained above)
2. There are no inferred entities: only experienced items can be claimed to exist

*Therefore*, there are no objects 'in themselves.'

Phenomenalists reject entities inferred from experiential clues in favor of entities constructed from experiential contents.[6] In failing to go along with the rejection of inferred entities (for reasons into which we cannot even enter here), we rebut the preceding argument by rejecting its second premiss.

It is important to stress (in particular as against certain fashionable tendencies in the interpretation of Kantian views) that our conceptual idealism is not phenomenalistic. We are not contending that the reality and persistence of physical objects inheres in the fact that human experiences occur regularly in certain systems. For if this were 'all there's to it,' if the systematicity of

---

[5] This argument is developed at greater length in Chap. XIII of N. Rescher, *The Coherence Theory of Truth* (Oxford, 1973).

[6] Compare Bertrand Russell: 'The supreme maxim in scientific philosophizing is this: *Whenever possible, logical constructions are to be substituted for inferred entities.*' (*Mysticism and Logic* [London, 1918], p. 155.) This quotation served as a motto for Rudolf Carnap's *Aufbau*.

experience were an *ultimate* fact, then we would have no account for it, or at best a strictly psychological account ('that's just how the mind does it'). But in fact we do have such an account available to us in principle, in terms of the corpus of scientific explanation that postulates a cluster of theories regarding an underlying reality of such-and-such a type (both as to the existence and the nature of the 'theoretical entities' by whose means the account proceeds). We have no reason to deny the *causal* primacy of the reality postulated in our scientific theorizing regarding the nature of the world – a primacy which, from the internal perspective of scientific theory, is altogether absolute. All that the conceptual idealist demands is that when we consider *externally* the mechanisms and terms of reference of our theorizing regarding reality (*qua* lawful, spatio-temporal, etc.), then we discern that it is articulated and mind-involving terms. Accordingly, conceptual idealism – unlike phenomenalism – is *not* a theory as to the structural nature of reality (this is left altogether to science), but addresses itself solely to the nature of the framework of concepts in terms of which this conception of the real is articulated. There is no reason why the conceptual idealist cannot accept the generic description of reality as we obtain it from scientific theorizing to represent a perfectly appropriate characterization of things as they really are 'in themselves.' What he does deny is that this description is given in mind-independent terms and that its 'objectivity' lies in a total exclusion of the element of mind.

Thus all three of these lines of argument against the possibility of at least *some* knowledge of (noumenal) objects 'in themselves' are insufficient to realize their objectives.

## 6. THE LEIBNIZIAN PERSPECTIVE: 'OUR REALITY' AS DEFINED INTRA-PHENOMENALLY

We have maintained that while the idea of a 'mind-independent reality' is not wholly vacuous in import, it represents a *via negativa* that really does not take us very far, and is in any case irrelevant for any information regarding 'our reality' (because radically discontinuous with it). But just what is involved in such a reorienting of 'reality' from the sphere of the altogether mind-independent towards that of an at least partly mind-conditioned truth? More must be said regarding the nature and the credentials of such a concept of reality not *an sich* but *for us*.

The position we espouse holds, with Kant, that *knowledge* of reality can be achieved only *within* the mind-conditioned sphere. But Kant felt driven to *postulate* a mind-inaccessible and in-principle-unknowable *Ding an sich* that must – despite its unknowability – be accepted in order to provide for the *objectivity* of man's disposition-reflecting experience. Our position altogether drops *this* kind of transcendental 'objectivity' in favour of a Leibnizian (and, so to speak, theory-internal) veridicality.[7] But with this mode of the veridical, 'true' does *not* mean 'true to an *sich* reality.' The line between dispositional appearance and reality is not to be drawn according to the equation

objectively true = corresponding with something altogether extra-theoretical

but rather according to the equation

objectively true = squaring with *everything* on the side of our warranted theorizing.

On this approach, one simply abandons the correspondence theory of reality built into the equivalence-thesis:

What the claim *P* asserts is really so = what *P* claims suitably corresponds to an altogether extra-theoretical state of affairs.

The 'real truth' of a thesis regarding reality must not be construed to require an intellectually unmanageable relation between what the thesis asserts and some *altogether extra*-theoretical, and so in principle cognitively inaccessible state of affairs. One cannot workably operate a correspondence theory with one inaccessible member: it is impossible to apply or implement. We must, in fact, abstain from any temptation to think of the relationship of our experience-based (and so dispositional) claims and *objective* (and

---

[7] I think here of Leibniz's splendid little essay *De modo distinguendi phaenomena realia ab imaginariis* in C. I. Gerhardt (ed.), *Philosophische Schriften*, vol. VIII (Berlin, 1890), pp. 219–20; tr. in L. E. Loemker, *Leibniz: Philosophical Papers and Letters* (Dordrecht, 1969), pp. 364–65.

so nondispositional and theory-abstractive) reality in terms of mapping: they are not maps, because they have no *pictorial* function whatsoever; they do not provide 'pictures of the terrain.' For this would require a separate term in a relation of representation, linking the represented reality with the representing conceptual instrument. A map embodies a conventional relation between a 'real thing' (e.g., a church) and its symbolic representative (the † marked on the sheet). With maps we can – and in principle must be able to – look outside the map and confront reality. This, of course, we cannot possibly do in the case in hand.

We are accordingly led to a *coherence theory of reality* that sees veridicality as lying in coherence. The 'is really true' is now not a matter of corresponding to an in-principle inaccessible mind-independent reality, but is determined wholly on the phenomenal side, as fitting in with everything we can learn about the world through observation and theory.[8]

From the earliest days of their subject, philosophers have made much of the contrast between appearance and reality inherent in the oft-encountered divergence between the actual facts and the subjective impressions of our observation of things in common experience. That a real world is in some fashion hidden away behind the world of phenomenal appearance, perhaps somehow manifesting itself through it, however dimly, to the discerning mind, is an idea as old as philosophy itself, and represents a theme central already in Greek philosophy from the Presocratics to Plato. The evolution of philosophical thought after Descartes showed with increasing clarity that this concept of appearance-underlying reality is something more and more crucial about which less and less can be said. With Kant, 'reality' is virtually back where it was in the days of the Greek skeptics as something altogether inaccessible to the human intellect.

But already with Leibniz,[9] the thesis is advanced that the bar-

[8] See N. Rescher, *The Coherence Theory of Truth* (Oxford, 1973).

[9] It seems to me that the vast group of more recent writers of empiricist affinity who see the distinction between reality and illusion to lie in the orderliness of the former has nothing essential to add to Leibniz's theory, except possibly for a probabilistic construction of the idea of order. (Cf. for example Hans Reichenbach, *Experience and Prediction* [Chicago, 1952].)

rier between appearance and reality should not be so drawn that reality is construed in strictly extra-phenomenal terms (reality = the sphere of what is extra-phenomenally the case); rather and more plainly, reality simply answers to *the truth* (reality = the sphere of what is 'really' [i.e., in fact] the case). On this view, reality is not an unattainable something that lies wholly outside the phenomenal realm, thanks to its *ex hypothesi* extra-mentalistic character. Rather 'reality' comes to be specified – nay, *defined* – *on the side of the dispositional appearances*, as comprising that sector of appearance that is *authentic*, factual, correct, or what have you. We come to the view adumbrated above that *reality* is to be understood not 'externally,' in terms of mind-independence, but 'internally,' in terms of what really and truly is the case from a standard, albeit mind-involving perspective. (Accordingly, we do not abandon a correspondence theory of truth, but merely endow it with a suitable interpretation.[10])

The contention is that reality-as-we-think-of-it (= *our* reality) is the only reality we can deal with, and that this is not mind-independent, but construed in mind-involving terms. And here 'mind-involving' does not imply 'idiosyncratic' or anywise subjective differing from one individual to another, like matters of opinion of taste or preference. For on the sense of 'objectivity' now in view, the appropriate equation is not objective = mind-independent (transcendental), but objective = interpersonally valid. On this view, 'reality' is not an absolute, but a universally accessible foundation framed within a communal conceptual scheme. Its conception is based on the publicly shared and interpersonally accessible determinate conceptual scheme, inherent in language, as a vehicle for interpersonal communication, and resides in such common conceptual resources as, preeminently, science.

---

[10] The truth of a factual proposition is now not a matter of an *isomorphic mapping* between its meaning-structure and an altogether thought-independent reality. The idea of a mapping-correspondence (with its impossible task of checking the accuracy of the map) is replaced by that of a representing-correspondence, where the marks of the adequacy of representation are purely internal to the propositional realm. For the working out of such a theory see N. Rescher, *The Coherence Theory of Truth, op. cit.*

Reality is thus not a mysterious unknowable something-or-other hidden away behind an impenetrable curtain. Rather, to differentiate between the real and the 'merely apparent' is to draw a distinction *within* the realm of experience itself (broadly construed to include the products of our theorizing). This view does not abandon the distinction between appearance and reality, but insists upon the propriety of a particular construction or interpretation of it. It sees reality not as transcendental, but as experientially immanent, due to its grounding in a conceptual scheme – an *experienced* world seen in fundamentally mind-invoking terms as a plurality of causally interacting space-time particulars. Accordingly, we are not endeavouring to gainsay the realm of real and objective fact, but refuse to construe this in altogether extra-theoretical terms, maintaining that 'the real' must inevitably be articulated by us from a theoretical perspective. Such a position refuses to fight the battle on the old ground as the search for an in principle unknowable something, and totally denies the need for any *Ding an sich* as a basis or presupposition for objective truth.

The futile search for a comprehensible something *outside* the sphere of what is possibly apprehensible in experience and theorizing is abandoned on this approach. To insist with Hegel that Kant is wrong and that real knowledge *must* somehow be a knowledge of things in themselves, that any 'knowledge' of phenomena is spurious since these are 'mere appearances,' is to fall afoul of a very fundamental point. For such a complaint ignores Leibniz's crucial *intra-phenomenal* distinction between the real (well-founded) and the illusory (ill-founded). On this view – essentially that of a Leibnizian idealism – the contrast between reality and appearance is not that between what is inside and what is outside the domain of 'phenomenally' accessible information: the contrast – properly understood – *is to be drawn wholly within this realm.*

To take this stance is, in effect, to abandon the correspondence theory of truth for a coherence theory, at any rate as far as an effective *criterion* is concerned, a working standard of truth-screening. One is led to take this line by considering that, as we have no theory-independent apprehension of reality, the best we can possibly do is to construct a coherent conceptual and theoretical scheme *about* reality.

But, given that actual 'correspondence to the extra-theoretical facts' is thus ruled out of the arena of actual epistemic practice, what considerations can possibly *legitimate* such a presupposition-laden scheme as correct (accurate, appropriate, or what have you)? Some sort of rational legitimation is clearly essential.

### 7. CONCEPT-DARWINISM AS A PRAGMATIC BASIS OF LEGITIMACY

The crucial question of the validity of 'our reality' remains to be dealt with. This question is perhaps best approached through the following objection: Why *should* the work of theorizing mind, as based on dispositional data, fit the real (nondispositional) facts? What validates our standard, disposition-based theoretical view of 'reality'?

A traditional correspondentist answer to this question of legitimation will not help at all. We cannot profitably argue 'Our concept of reality is legitimate because it (actually) corresponds to "authentic reality".' This line of argument runs into the roadblock posed by the question: just what manner of 'reality' is at issue in this correspondence? (1) Is it reality *an sich* construed in altogether mind-independent terms? That reply won't do, because how could one possibly support it? (2) Is it reality-as-we-think-it? Of course a corespondence obtains here, but that is just trivial (circular); so this response does not provide any answer, and furnishes no rationale whatever for the requisite legitimation.

Given these shortcomings of the correspondentist approach to the criterion of reality, we have turned in another direction and taken the coherentist route, adopting as our standard of 'the ← real truth' the best theoretical systematization of our experience. But this only raises, and does not settle, the issue of legitimation.

The critical step is to recognize that the question 'Why do our ← conceptual mechanisms fit "the real world" with which we interact intellectually?' simply does not permit of any purely aprioristic answer on strictly theoretical grounds of general principle. Rather, it is to be answered in basically the same way as the question: 'Why do our bodily mechanisms fit the world with which we interact physically?' <u>Both</u> are alike to be resolved in essentially Darwinian evolutionary terms.

The 'standard conceptual framework' for structuring our view of reality – our categorical perspective upon things and the intellectual mechanisms by which we form our view of 'the way the world works' – are built up by an historic, evolutionary process in terms of 'trial and error,' exactly as with the bodily mechanisms by which we comport ourselves in the physical world. These conceptions accordingly develop subject to revision in terms of 'success and failure' as determined by means of standards themselves defined by the norms of the enterprise of rational inquiry. The concept of a 'governing purpose' here serves as a regulative guide – just as with any other goal-oriented human activity.

The evolutionary development of categorial and descriptive frameworks proceeds by natural selection. As changes come to be entertained (within our civilization), it transpires that one is 'better' than another in terms of its fitness to survive, because it answers better to the range of purposes at issue. A conceptual scheme is an instrument for organizing our experience into a systematized view of reality. It is an instrumentality, an operational code, a set of instructions for operating in the context of our life-environment. And as with any tool or instrument, the question of evaluation takes the form of a pragmatic assessment: Does it work? Does it produce the desired results? Is it successful in practice? The central issue is a matter of 'survival of the fittest' with *fitness* assessed in terms of the practical objectives of the rational enterprise. Legitimation is found in substantial part in the fact of survival through historical vicissitudes. This subordination of theory to practice in the domain of rationality as understood in the Western tradition derived from the Greeks points to a *pragmatic* aspect of the theory which must be analyzed in detail. The pivotal issue is that of 'working out best.'

But what does 'best' mean here? This carries us back to the Darwinian perspective of the preceding discussion. A Darwinian legitimation clearly requires a standard of 'fitness.' There are a *variety* of conceptual schemes regarding 'how things work in the world.' The examples of such occult explanatory frameworks as those of numerology (with its benign ratios), astrology (with its astral influences), and black magic (with its mystic forces) indicate that alternative explanatory frameworks exist, and that these can have very diverse degrees of merit. Now the governing standards of the Western tradition of human rationality are presented by the goals of *explanation*, *prediction*, and *control*. (And thus not, for example, sentimental 'at-oneness with nature.' Thus think of the magician vs. the mystic vs. the sage as cultural ideal.) We want to argue here that this standard is provided by considerations of *practice* and is inherent in the use to which conceptual schemes are put in the management of our affairs in the conduct of life. In the Western intellectual tradition the ultimate standards of rationality are defined by a very basic concept of knowledge-wed-to-practice, and their ultimate validation lies in the combination of theoretical and practical *success*.

Such a pragmatic-evolutionary answer to the question of the legitimation of the standard conceptual scheme involves our frequently Kantian position in yet another of its departures from Kant. Kant saw the legitimation of the standard framework of concepts in his 'deduction' of the categories, and regarded this validation as given in altogether *a priori* terms of reference to the inevitable preconditions of objective experience. His method was heavily presuppositional: 'If our experience is to attain to objective validity, then its conformity to the categories must be realized.' He took the source of the conformity of our knowledge with the categories to derive ultimately from the transcendental conditions of the possibility of objective experience-based knowledge of things within the realm of nature.

By contrast, our present position can lay claim to no such all-out justification resting 'on general principles.' As we see it, the standard conceptual scheme is simply one alternative among others, and has no inevitable foothold in the very constitution of the faculty-structure of the human intellect. Our legitimation is accordingly not *a priori* and absolute, but merely *a posteriori* and relative. The merit of the scheme lies in its having established itself in open competition with its rivals and having shown – on the basis of the historical vagaries of a Darwinian process of selection – that it works out in actual practice. Such a legitimation is not absolute, but only presumptive – the product rather of a democratic struggle among rival candidates than a making good of the elevated claims of an eighteenth-century absolute monarch. But it does, in its Darwinian aspect, give some justificatory weight to the historical factor of being in *de facto* possession.

In this sense *practice* is the arbiter of theory. And in place of a Kantian 'deduction' our present legitimation of the standard scheme takes the form of a conceptualistic pragmatism. *Pragmatism* enters in because we seek validation in the assessment of 'what works out'; and it is a *conceptualistic* version of this approach because conceptual schemes are at issue. Thus in the final analysis we take the validation of *the objectivity of the standard framework of mind-involving concepts* to lie not in their 'actually corresponding to rigoristically mind-independent reality' (which they *in principle* could not do), but in their providing the cognitive instruments by which we can effectively manage our practical affairs and successfully find our way about in the world.

# Chapter X

# IDEALISTIC THEORY OF MIND

## 1. MIND AS BASIC

As has repeatedly been stressed, idealism need not, and our idealism does not, take the form of spiritualism or panpsychism; it need not and does not maintain that *only minds exist* and that all there is is somehow the product of mind. Accordingly, our idealism does not hold that mind is basic in any productive or causative sense. Rather, the idealist position espoused here sees mind as *conceptually* basic; that is, as basic in the conceptual mode of explanatory analysis, providing in various respects the *conceptual paradigm* for the constitution of the categories in terms of which we think about things. For example, we have maintained that mind-endowed individuals (= *persons*) may be seen as paradigmatic for the conception of *particulars* in general, and that mind-inaugurated agency (= the *actions* of people) may be seen as paradigmatic for the generalized concept of *causation*. The conceptualistic idealism here articulated thus maintains the primacy of mind as a model for the constituting of the view of the world operative in our standard conceptual scheme. Such a position rests heavily on the rationalist thesis that mind does not reflect reality in a somehow invariant, mirror-like, passive and non-contributory way, but contributes actively and *transactionally* to the constitution – as well as the constituting – of our knowledge of reality. However, our position also extends beyond such rationalism in holding that the mind makes this contribution *in its own terms*, by its deployment of concepts relying upon mentalistic conceptions and paradigms. This last-indicated view amounts to idealism proper – albeit of an essentially conceptual sort. The conceptualistic idealist sees mind as an explicative paradigm in the conceptual order of analytical understanding rather than as a productive source in the causal order of genetic explanation. This position does not see mind as the productive source of reality; but sees it – commonsensically enough – as the productive source of our knowledge of reality, though proceeding to insist that the mind plays this productive role in such a way as to make a formative contribution to the shaping of the end-product, *reality as we know it* (in contradistinction to reality as it is 'in itself').

One recent writer defines idealism as 'the attempt or claim "to interpret reality in terms of mind".'[1] This formula is ambiguous (as is appropriate for the encapsulation of a many-faceted doctrine). It might be construed *spiritualistically*, as saying that 'the real world' is mind-like – that the stuff that composes it is somehow mental or that nature is itself somehow one vast hypermind. This certainly is not our view. Again, it might be construed *phenomenalistically*, as saying that mind is the author of nature in a way akin to the poet's authorship of his poem: as a purely intellectual construction, the essentially fictive creation of the mind drawing solely upon resources of its own. This too is certainly not our view. Finally, it could be construed *conceptually*, as holding that the ideas and categories in terms of and by means of which our view of reality is articulated are in essential part framed by the mind in its own terms, with reference to its own capacities, capabilities, and modes of operation. This last construal represents our own position, and exactly specifies the mode of idealism articulated here.

## 2. AN IDEALIST VIEW OF MIND

Our idealism views mind from a functional angle, focussing upon *what it does*. On this approach, the basic question regarding minds is not *structural* (of what and in what manner they are constituted) or *causal* (relating to the productive origins of minds), but *functional*, giving the prime stress to the paradigmatic role of *what minds do* (or more properly, *what they can do*), this being regarded from a phenomenological or analytical, rather than an explanatory or causal point of view. The theory views the mind in terms of its characteristic activities, as operative agent with respect to a vast group of coordinated abilities, capabilities, and

[1] Charles Hartshorne, 'The Case for Idealism,' *The Philosophical Forum*, vol. 1 (1968), pp. 7–23.

powers: sensing (seeing, hearing, etc.), imagining, hypothesizing, dreaming, calculating, etc. The items of such a schedule of definitively mental activities provides for us the essential entry points into the realm of mind. At this level, humans need not, of course, exercise an absolute monopoly. But the point is that if we describe the acts of a robot or creature from outer space as calculating (rather than performing numerical manipulations) or as talking (rather than as issuing sounds), then the very terminology we employ decisively prejudices or settles through its inherent presuppositions the question of whether or not the thing in view has a mind.

In saying that idealism views mind in its generic aspect with a view not to particular minds but to *mind-in-general*, we are not espousing some theory of a universalistic world-mind. Our position risks no self-damage in rejecting any reference to a world-soul, cosmic-spirit, super-mind, or any sort of person-transcending intelligence. It can reject all this with impunity and proceed on the rather more prosaic road of individual people and their minds, establishing whatever degree of community, mutuality, interpersonal accord and objectivity is wanted (and a great deal *is* wanted) through language and the publicly shared conceptual mechanisms that its instrumentalities render available.

These considerations point the way by which our theory proposes to confront a Kantian difficulty that has exercised interpreters of the *Critique of Pure Reason* throughout the years. I have in mind the problem – with which Adamson, Kemp Smith, and Prichard (among others) have struggled – of how men experience a *common* world of objects, given that Kant is apparently entitled by his own theory to no more than that each of us has his own personal (and so, for all we know, *idiosyncratic*) forms for experiencing the products of sense and thought. It is clear that X's own personal experience (of . . . does it even deserve the name of a publicly observed world?) is nowise identical or overlapping with Y's own personal experience. And so how can it be assured on Kantian grounds that the inherent *forms* of these disjoint bodies of experience are identical, so that these individuals jointly share and communicate about a *common* world. In abandoning straightforward realism, does the idealist not destroy the basis for legitimation of a shared, public, and 'objective' world – at any rate short of enlisting the services of a Berkeleyan *deus ex machina*? This family of issues revolving around the factors of objectivity and community that underly *communication* are at the center of the problem-cluster that faces any idealist theory of mind. To these difficulties conceptual idealism offers a characteristic and straightforward reply.

Mind has two aspects: process and content, capability and performance, potential and actualization. The former – process – relates to the capabilities generic to minds in general. The latter – content – relates to the specific, idiosyncratic, biographical performances that take place within the generic framework of these capabilities: the specific seeings, hypotheses, calculations, and the like, of particular persons. The communal capabilities and functions of minds are operative through procedural mechanisms that are generic, public, shared; the performances of minds are person-relative and pertinent to specific individuals and occasions.

This character of the mind as an instrument or agency of conceptualization possessed of a complex of characteristic capabilities is the aspect crucial to our present view. Our conceptual idealism is articulated with reference to capability and instrumentality rather than performance. It takes the view that it is only to be expected that our personal experience of mental processes should find their communal expression in the public language we use to talk and think about the world. And such mental operations take place within a public and interpersonal framework that has its articulation in such social resources as a language, its conceptual scheme, and the underlying *Weltanschauung*.

Our theory thus does not replace publicly shared reality by private imagining or wishful thinking. It is developed with reference to the mind-invoking aspects of concepts as embedded in language, concepts that are thus public in nature in two respects: (1) in their *basis*, which resides in a shared social instrumentality, viz., language and its associated conceptual scheme, and (2) in their *reference*, which relates to the common, generic capabilities of minds. In this way, our idealism concerns itself not with the psychological and personal, but with the conceptual and public. Our view of mind stresses the naturalness of the use of mind-invoking concepts by beings for whom mental performance represents a massively prominent sector of first-hand experience.

The mind is seen from this angle as an agency that disposes over a system of characteristic capabilities. Accordingly, what is at issue when we speak of 'the mind' is not the individual accomplishments of particular minds but the generic capabilities within the reach of people-in-general. The humanly contrived vehicles of communication inherent in language suffice to provide the requisite objectivity for our conceptualistic idealism. We need not go the lengths of an idealism of Absolute or capital-S Spirit: the socially established communicative resources that are the common resource of individual minds can and do suffice wholly for our purposes. The theory does not call for supplementing the commonplace plurality of individual minds by a *deus-ex-machina* supermind: it merely requires due stress not only on the doings of particular minds but on the instrumentalities common to minds in general – above all, those relating to communication.

On this approach, then, it is seen as the characteristic and natural province of mind to preside over certain capacities and capabilities that endow it with the resources requisite for interpersonal communication – viz. language and its implicit conceptual scheme. These functions are communal and public in their very nature, since what is at issue is communication, and its linguistic/conceptual apparatus is an inherently social and interpersonal activity. The *conceptual* orientation of our idealism thus circumvents the Kantian difficulty of establishing the public availability of the forms of perception and thought. It locates the source of these cognitive forms squarely in the sphere of those quintessentially social and interpersonal resources afforded by languages and their conceptual apparatus.

To be sure, some Kant-reminiscent questions still lurk unanswered in the background: how is the sharing by diverse minds of a common language and conceptual scheme possible? How is a socially communal mechanism for public communication regarding a presumptively shared world possible?

Our theory (as usual) finds the roots of possibility in the actual, holding that in the final analysis these possibilities derive from a matter of fact. Mind-endowed creatures (i.e. people) simply have

N

certain (Darwinianly originated) capabilities for language learning and concept-acquisition, capacities that provide the basis for
communication as well as other publicly shared patterns of social
behavior. That people have these capacities is a matter of brute
fact – one that admits, as facts generally do, of *scientific explanation* (along essentially evolutionary lines), but does not admit, and
presumably does not *need*, any philosophical rationalization.
How it comes about – in terms of an adequate scientific account
– that minds possess the capacity of developing concepts through
the use of language is certainly a long story, and one articulated
but imperfectly at this day. But there is no reason for us to await
in silence the end of its telling. For the key fact about minds from
the angle of the needs and purposes of our conceptual idealism is
simply *that* they have these capabilities; the mechanism-oriented
question of *how* it comes to be that they have them is an issue
which, however interesting in itself, is for present purposes superfluous.

### 3. THE ROLE OF IMPUTATION

It is natural enough that our understanding of things should be
formed within a conceptual framework replete with mind-
referential terms, reflecting the role of mind as a general paradigm, operative even with respect to the range of what is
(seemingly) extra-mental. Conceptual idealism thus holds that
many of our key concepts are originally articulated on the basis
of mentalesque paradigms, but then unhesitatingly applied over a
far wider range. This is typically and generically accomplished
through the projective process characterized as *imputation* in the
analysis of lawfulness (in Chap. IV). Conceptual idealism finds
this process to be prominent throughout the categories of
the standard conceptual scheme: possibility/necessity, causality
and control, the constituting of ordering frameworks of space and
time, etc. The sort of imputation at issue here is a characteristic
resource of minds which provides the mechanisms of concept-
formation that operate throughout the domain of conceptual
idealism.

This imputational theory dispels the mystery of how one is

able to go beyond observation even in cases where orthodox inductive procedures are obviously unsuitable or irrelevant. It is useful to consider some further examples of this phenomenon, going beyond the (by now familiar) case of lawfulness.

*Case 1: Appearance and Reality.* Observation is confined to appearance, to dealing with the looks and smells (etc.) of things. But how things look to us, smell to us, etc., is patently person-relative and relative to appearances. It is by *imputation* that we effect the move from 'seems' to 'is', so as to take us well beyond what a thing seems to be and what we take it to be and arrive at what it 'is really like' (at least purportedly).

*Case 2: Other Minds.* Consider the traditional 'problem of other minds.' One's *observational* evidence regarding other people is always restricted to observation of manifest behavior. But *mind*, of course, has to do with (1) power/ability/capability and (2) the unobservably private and publicly inaccessible purely 'mental' concomitants of overt behavior. It is by imputation that we move beyond manifest behavior to the mental states of others.

*Case 3: Powers/Abilities/Capabilities.* Observation is limited to *performance*, to what a thing (or person) in fact does on specific occasions. Its powers and their congeners do not lie open to public view. Here again, it is by imputation that we move beyond overt actual doings to the implicit powers, dispositions, abilities (etc.) of things.

*Case 4: Teleology and Purpose.* Our observational experience relates only to overt goings-on. It is again by imputation that we move beyond them to the realm of aims and purposes.

All such cases conform to the same basic paradigm. Observational evidence is *in principle* insufficient to establish the claims built into our concepts. One encounters, throughout, the standard aspect of all evidential situations that the actual evidence in hand is (always and necessarily) insufficient to warrant the claim based upon it. Nor can the gap be breached by an 'inductive' step (because in induction the evidence is *homogenous* with its extensions: we move from given cases of a certain sort to other, inaccessible cases *of just that same sort*).

The evidential gap is bridged by an *imputation*. Observation provides not *evidence*, but *cues and clues* on the basis of which we cognitively assimilate observationally inaccessible cases to others that lie open to first-hand experience, proceeding to subsume them under a common rule. Cases with which we have first-hand familiarity (our minds, our powers, our observational resources, etc.) are accordingly taken as *paradigmatic* bases for constructing an interpersonal sector of experience that combines other cases with those of which we have such familiarity of first-hand experience. We construct a framework of concepts for which mentalistic paradigms are crucial, but once constructed, do not hesitate to deploy it over a far wider terrain. Such imputational projection provides a means of filling in and rounding off our understanding by furnishing a basis for the use of a conceptual scheme that projects the application of concepts arrived at in the familiar setting of first-hand experience beyond the limits of this initial range. In all such situations, we apply mind-oriented models in a (contextually) *a priori* manner, since they are not *extracted from* the experiential evidence of the cases in hand but rather *projected into* it. Our concepts reflect – or rather formalize – this projective or imputational functioning of certain mind-relativized models or paradigms. The key point of our position is that just such imputationally laden concepts are standardly deployed in the cognitive organization of physical stimuli into rationally structured and meaningful units of experience. (The historically oriented reader may here find it helpful to think of a comparison with Kant's 'Deduction of the Categories.')

The standard framework for thinking about natural reality is replete with such evidence-transcending ingredients. And, as we have argued, the very language in which we talk about the sphere of 'extra-mental' nature is laden with concepts that go beyond not only what the observed evidence is, but what, 'objectively speaking,' it *could* be, because of their invocation of mentalistic paradigms. The noormorphic aspect of our conceptual scheme is clearly manifest from this perspective.

The imputation at issue is not personal and idiosyncratic: its ground-rules are a matter of public property. It is not a personal act but a public resource built into a social framework, based upon a communally available conceptual scheme as enshrined in language.[2]

A cluster of imputations (or bases for imputation) is built into the very foundations of our conceptual scheme. Our *concepts* are designed to work in such a way that the seemingly unwarranted claim is rationally warranted because 'that's what's being said': the conceptual scheme embodies a 'theoretical' stance towards the world that embodies (and is the product of) certain imputations. Causes, material objects, persons, all represent theoretical entities within a framework for organizing our thought about things. They are the conceptual *vehicles for imputation*. In a perhaps overly Kantian terminology, the application of such imputationally laden concepts might be characterized as conceptually immanent though empirically transcendent.

But if all these standardly applied conceptions step beyond their evidential base and are *not* justified by *inductive* considerations, then how are they to be justified at all? They are justified *by articulation through a conceptual scheme that is in turn entrenched on Darwinian grounds and validated through pragmatic considerations.* The evolutionary development of symbolic processes and conceptual schemes provides the key to rational validation here. Along lines exactly parallel with those articulated in the preceding chapter, we can invoke an evolutionary pragmatism to justify a conceptual framework whose concepts have a semantical meaning-content that goes beyond what the basis of their application is or indeed could possibly be.

---

[2] Our theory of imputations has definite points of similarity with the Theory of Fictions of Hans Vaihinger's *The Philosophy of 'As If'* (tr. C. K. Ogden [New York, 1924].) But there are crucial points of difference. Vaihinger's fictions are overt assumptions rather than tacitly covert models – and so they are explicit theses rather than representing conceptually implicit relationships; they are 'assumptions made with a full realization of the impossibilities of the thing assumed' (p. 90). Moreover, Vaihinger sees his fictions as part of 'the subjective logical scaffolding of thought' (p. 105) whose status is always that of an explicit falsehood (an 'expedient error,' p. 108). From our standpoint the status of imputations is cognitively regulative, and they thus lack the explicit falsehood of a constitutive thesis that perpetrates a substantive error.

## 4. THE NOOMORPHIC CONCEPTION OF MIND

As stated above, our conceptual idealism views mind from a *functional* perspective, focussing upon what minds do. Its model of mind is neither of the 'black-box' type (with a view only to inputs and outputs and no concern with what stands in between) nor of the 'cybernetic' type (with a wholly externalized analysis of the structures required to effect certain mentalistic functions). Rather, our model is unabashedly *anthropomorphic*, in that, being ourselves mind-endowed creatures, we need not reconstruct the phenomenology of mental experience by inference from external observation, but, since *we are able to experience it for ourselves*, are in a position to construct our view of it 'from within,' so to speak. Whatever be the status of the 'mind' *per se*, such 'mental operations' as sensing, imagining, calculating, etc., represent processes that lie within the range of the first-hand familiarity of direct experience. Since we are familiar with the phenomenology of mental performance in the setting of our first-hand experience, this can serve as basis for understanding the processes of mind *on their own terms*. This model of mind does not look to mechanical devices or computing machines, but to minds as we are familiar with them in our own common experience. One may thus characterize it as a *noomorphic* model: a theory of mental performance based upon our first-hand experience of mental phenomena and incorporated in our standard ways of talking not only about them, but extended, by by projection, over a far wider range.[3]

On such a noomorphic view of mind, our understanding of mental processes comes 'from within' – thanks to the fact that we are ourselves the performing agents of mental acts. Accordingly, when we conceive of mental operations on our usual conceptual scheme, we do not think in terms of inputs and outputs, or even of the accomplishment of certain functional transformations, but in terms of such familiar performances as worrying, planning, think-

[3] The position of this paragraph, with its emphasis on the first-hand experience of our characteristic mental powers, is indebted to Rom Harré, both as to Chapters 8 and 10 of his *The Principles of Scientific Thinking* (London, 1970) and also discussions regarding yet unpublished materials.

ing, etc. Such a theory of mind roots in the soil of those performances which are so familiar in our characteristically mental activities that we take them altogether for granted in the communicative use of language: the apprehension of meanings as operative in the object-directed (intensional) use of words and the interpretation of sentences and statement-complexes.

These considerations point to the crucial difference between the explanatory and the hermeneutic aspect of a theory of mind. The task of the former is to explain why and how, and its concern is accordingly with the essentially causal character of the explanatory enterprise. The task of the latter is essentially descriptive and phenomenological, its aim being to characterize what goes not *causally*, but *explicatively*, providing an essentially analytical understanding in terms of meanings and intensions. Not the *how-mechanisms* of language-use as an instrumentality of overt behavior ('linguistic behaviour'), but the *why-teleology* inherent in the purposive meaning-oriented dimension of communication, are the central concerns of the hermeneutic enterprise.

The explanatory mission is generally discharged in terms of talk about the physico-chemical processes operative in physical structures (cogwheels, clockworks, etc. on the old atomistic model; electromagnetic mechanisms like neuron firings on the modern neurophysiological model), or else in terms of the transformational language of input and output, or the causal language of stimulus and response. Such explanatory models may in their own way be perfectly correct, and may well be wholly adequate to the discharge of their proper explanatory mission. They may well characterize entirely adequately and comprehensively the mechanism-directed 'how?' and the causal 'why?' of the occurrence of mental transactions. Still, all these *explanatory* models leave out something no less crucial, interesting, and important, because they do not characterize what happens in its internal, intensional, hermeneutic dimension. And they cannot do so, not because of any internal shortcomings, but because they are cast in altogether different terms of reference, since the purposive aspect is simply another *dimension* of language use, articulated in different terms from those of the causal aspect.

These considerations are critical for an understanding of our position. For they enable our conceptual idealism to face and resolve a line of objection to which the traditional forms of idealism were vulnerable. This is the objection inherent in the question:

> But what becomes of this idealistic mentalism if it transpires that one can explain the workings and performances of mind itself physico-chemically or in some other essentially causal way?

The anwer, in briefest outline is: *Nothing* happens, because our idealism is not conceived along *explanatory* lines at all (neither ontologically nor causally − it envisages mind neither as the stuff nor the cause of extra-mental things), but along *explicative*, that is conceptual and hermeneutic, lines. This important issue cries out for a fuller and more detailed analysis.

### 5. IDEALISM AND MATERIALISM:
### MIND AND THE CAUSAL ORDER

The conceptualistic idealism articulated here thus does not need to be argued through an attack upon causal materialism. And there is actually no need for a conceptual idealist to deny that mental functioning has its material basis in the realm of physical process. When everything needful has been said in support of the present view, the prospect is still open that minds are *causally* dependent on the physical operations of matter. What has been maintained is that the world-as-we-conceive-it (even if we are materialists) is conceived by us by means of concepts that are fundamentally mind-invoking. The idealism articulated here has been developed in terms of a mind-involvement that is construed along conceptual and presuppositional lines; nothing whatever has been said about any sort of dependencies that might be at issue on the side of the scientific explanation in terms of physical causality.

This state of affairs leaves the position we have advanced open to being overbid by a materialism prepared to argue as follows:

> Have it your way. Let material particulars (whose very conception requires reference to particularity, space and time, and

causality) be mind-involving along the conceptual lines you have argued. But there is nothing in all this that conflicts with a materialist position holding that minds themselves are matter-derivative, with the consequence that the whole range of the mental is itself to be accounted for by an explanation given in terms of the material, perhaps partly along causal lines, partly along the lines of an identity theory.

The materialist who argues in this way is quite right. Nothing in the dialectic of the present discussion forecloses this prospect that the sort of mind-involvement in question is only one half of the story, in that the mental element on whose role the idealist insists is itself somehow reducible to or emergent from the material within the order of causation (or of explanation) in physical science. Indeed, even in the most extreme case of seeming divergence, a reconciliation of the 'conflicting' positions is possible. For consider the outright juxtaposition of

1. An idealism that insists that matter and causality are conceptually mind-dependent.
2. A materialism that insists that minds are causally dependent upon matter.

Even here, in this extreme case of apparently dramatic opposition, there is in fact no insuperable conflict and no vicious circularity, since *wholly different modes of dependence* are at issue in the two cases.

It is crucially important to keep in mind the clear and far-reaching distinction between *conceptual* involvement or invocation on the one hand and *causal* involvement or invocation on the other. Raw materials (flour, sugar, etc.) are *causally* requisite for the cake: they must be in hand before the physical process of cake-production can get under way. But there is nothing in the *concept* of a cake that says it must be made in this way: it is possible, at least in theory, that cake could be made of very different stuff. And thus these ingredients are not called for in the conceptual order: the concept of cake is not essentially flour-referring as that of a raisin is grape-referring (since raisins simply *are* dried grapes). Conceptual interrelationships derive from the meanings of concepts, and thus manifest the hermeneutic connections inherent in logico-semantical linkages. The causal order is not capable of this sort of rationalization. Here – wholly outside the range of actual meaning-connections – there is room for genuine surprise. A thing can be linked *causally* to virtually anything else (caterpillars and butterflies; cigarette smoking and cancer).

The analytical order of a hermeneutic exposition of meanings is altogether detached from the causal order of scientific explanation.[4] Causal connections are void of any inner linkages of necessity, meaning-connection or the like. In the causal sphere one can *explain* mechanisms of correlation, but one cannot discern any relationships of inherent intelligibility. As Hume incisively and decisively argued, physico-causal connections can do no more than achieve *familiarity* in repeated experience, but never *intelligibility*, and their epistemic basis is in observation rather than pure thought. But meaning-connections, unlike causal connections, are matters of pure intelligibility and emerge from analysis rather than from experience.

This difference in the *terms of reference* at issue is crucial for our purposes. The conceptual idealism presented here has not addressed itself at all to the explanatory aspect of mental performances. Our discussion has been concerned with the mind-invoking dimension of the content of our concepts in their hermeneutic aspect, even those concepts critical for the very description of the material world (space, time, causality). The range of issues relating to explanations given in the causal mode have remained altogether outside our analytical purview. The conceptual idealist has no vested interest in arguing that mind and its functioning are not somehow causally emergent from the processes of matter. His point is simply that our standard rational account of the world – its material sector specifically included – is given in terms of reference that are at bottom mind-involving. It is the analytical issue of *how* we think of the world, not the explanatory issue of its causal goings-on, that constitutes the focus of concern.

---

[4] This crucial fact was unfortunately kept out of sight during a long period of philosophical history by the dual role of the Latin *causa* in serving for *reason* in the intelligible mode and as efficient *cause* in the casual mode.

Thus the idealist thesis that one specific direction of dependence (viz., that of the physical upon that of the mental) is built into our standard conceptual scheme must not – I think – be construed as in principle conflicting with the debatable (but by no means thereby negligible) prospect that the order of scientific explanation might lead to positing a reversal in the direction of dependence.

At this point comes the following objection:

> All this is surely just mere sophistry. This position foists upon us a double-truth theory akin to medieval Averroism or the near-Averroism of Kant. For, like Kant, you are in effect saying that one gets one sort of story on the part of *theoretical* reason (or rather here: the explanatory framework of science) and another, conflicting theory on the part of *practical* reason (or rather here: the conceptual analysis of ideational frameworks).

This objection is quite erroneous. There just is no question of any real conflict when the proper distinctions have been drawn, because quite different things are at issue in the two cases. When different perspectives are involved, seemingly conflicting theses are perfectly compatible. (I can say without conflict that my car is economical in point of gas mileage and uneconomical in point of maintenance costs.) The point is that altogether different sorts of dependencies or requirements are operative in the two theses:

1. that mind is *causally* dependent upon (i.e., causally requires) matter, in that mental process demands *causally* or productively the physical workings of matter.
2. that matter (conceived of in the standard manner of material substance subject to physical law) is *explicatively* dependent upon (i.e., *conceptually* requires) mind, in that the conception of material processes involves *hermeneutically* or semantically the mentalistic workings of mind.

We must here keep in view once again the crucial distinction between the conceptual order with its essentially hermeneutic or *explicative* perspective upon the intellectual exposition of meanings, and the *causal* order with its *explanatory* perspective upon the causal rationalization of physical processes. In the hermeneutic framework of consideration, our concern is not with any facets of the causal explanation of intellectual processes, but upon understanding them from within, on their own terms. The issue is not one of *causal explanation* at all, but one of the *understanding* to be achieved through an analysis of the internal meaning-content of concepts and of the semantical *information* conveyed by statements in which they are operative. Because of the fundamental difference between these two perspectives, any conflict in the dependency relations to which they give rise is altogether harmless from the standpoint of actual inconsistency. For once all the due distinctions are duly heeded any semblance of conflict between the two opposed modes of priority disappears. No doubt, this calls for a certain amount of care and subtlety – but then so do many issues of intellectual life, and why should things be easier in philosophy than elsewhere?

Accordingly, the pivotal fact merits emphasis that the analysis given here is in no way invalidated if a materialist approach is taken with respect to the issue of the 'causal' origins of mind. For the whole mechanism of such an approach, with its basic reliance on space, time, causality, and individuated objects, is shot through with conceptions which – if our preceding analysis has any merit – are fundamentally mind-involving.

But even if one grants the preceding point, and concedes that a materialist theory of mind in not *inconsistent* with our idealist position, would its adoption not generate a vicious circle of the following form?

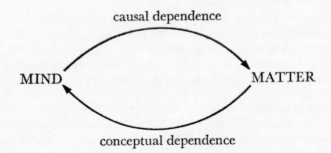

The answer to this question is negative. For as the diagram itself indicates, the circle is not vicious since *different* modes of dependency are involved. The circle breaks because we traverse its two halves in altogether different ways: from mind to matter in the conceptual order of understanding (of *rationes cognoscendi* or rather *concipiendi*); from matter to mind in the explanatory order of causation (*rationes essendi*).

The present idealistic view is that the sphere of matter is mind-involving in that the concept of material objects, located in space and time and interacting with one another, is shot through with mind-invoking conceptions. But this entire argument that mind is basic for matter is carried through in the conceptual order. On our explanation of the matter, a mind-invoking conception is one whose ultimate-analysis demands a reference to minds or their capabilities. The 'mentalistic' or mind-referring sector of a conceptual framework is accordingly spanned by those of its conceptions whose rational exposition can only be accomplished in ultimately mind-invoking terms, that is, by means of concepts relating to characteristically mental capabilities. Nothing is said here about any priority of mind over matter in the causal order. Our position has left open entirely the prospect that mind could hinge on matter in point of causation.

But even if no vicious circle arises, do we not arrive at an equally vicious infinite regress that altogether precludes understanding – that is, if an adequate understanding of mind requires reference to its causal origins in matter and an adequate understanding of matter requires reference to its functional presuppositions of a mind-invoking sort? The answer is No – no vicious regress is involved. Such a regress would arise only if one adopted an essentially linear model of understanding. But this is quite inappropriate in the case of *coordinated* concepts such as the present instance of mind/matter or the simpler case of cause/effect. To say that we cannot fully understand the cause until we understand its effect, and that we cannot fully understand the effect until we understand the cause, is not to show that there is a vitiating regress with the result that we cannot understand either one. All it shows is that two such coordinated and interrelated concepts cannot be set out through a *sequential* explanation but must be grasped *together* in their systematic unity. An analogy may help. Take a knife and its blade. If that object is to count as a knife, then that shiny thing attached to the handle must be a blade, but this thing cannot count as a blade unless the whole it comprises together with that handle is a knife. The two items stand in conceptually symbiotic apposition: $X$ cannot be properly characterized as $X$ unless it is duly related to $Y$ and $Y$ cannot be properly characterized as such unless it is duly related to $X$. We cannot pick up either end of the stick in separation from the other, but must grasp the whole in one fell swoop. Just such a cognitive *coordination* of mentalistic and materialistic concepts holds with respect to our present analysis of their mutual interdependencies. By maintaining a sufficient set of due distinctions, any collapse into vicious circularity or vitiating regress can be avoided.

Idealism holds that mind is fundamental *vis à vis* material reality (as we understand it). But our conceptual idealism specifies that this fundamentality in the *conceptual* order, not in that of a *causal* idealism (such as that of Berkeley) maintaining that matter – insofar as it being at all – is the phenomenal *product* of the working of minds.[5] The considerations of the preceding account show that such a conceptualistic idealism, which regards mind as basic to matter in the conceptual order, is even compatible with a causal materialism that maintains matter to be basic to mind in the causal order. On the causal issues of the origins of mind, conceptualistic idealism is silent and so compatible with various theories – materialism itself not excluded. Conceptual idealism just is not an *explanatory* theory regarding the causal mechanisms of the mind's processes or mode of origination; it is an *analytical* theory regarding the nature of the conceptual mechanisms of the categories of understanding. It can thus coexist with *any* theory of mind that is articulated along strictly *causal* lines, be it a materialistic view that sees the causal origin of mind in matter or a Cartesian-style dualism of reciprocal influence or even an epi-

[5] One must understand 'phenomenal product' here not in the sense of appearances to minds – for this implies that there is something extramental that does the appearing – but in the sense of what the mind 'takes to appear,' so that the begging of crucial questions can be avoided.

phenomenalism. Indeed, so far as the issue of interpretative understanding based on a meaning-directed analysis of concepts is concerned, we can *ignore* for all practical purposes the material foundations that figure so centrally when causal explanation is at issue.

But what of an 'identity theory of mind' that *identifies* mental processes with the operation of certain material configurations, viz., brains? Is our conceptual idealism not incompatible with such a theory? Not necessarily. It depends upon whether the identity is seen as a factual one (like the identity of the morning star with the evening star or that of the tallest man in the room with the poorest man in the room), or as a conceptually necessary one (like that of Smith's only brother with Smith's only male sibling). Our idealism will encounter no difficulties with a thesis of *contingent* identity. An incompatibility will arise only if the identity theory of the mental with the material is taken to obtain in *conceptual* terms, as holding the essentially concept-relative thesis that mentalistic talk is *eliminable*, in that it can be *translated without conceptually viable residue* into talk about the behavior of matter. Such a conceptually eliminative reductionism is incompatible with a conceptual idealism. For if 'mentalese' were analytically altogether reducible to materialistic discourse, then mind could not be conceptually basic to matter in the sense of our theory. But, of course, since our theory is based on an analysis of the *ordinary* conceptual scheme, this goes no further than to show that this ordinary scheme is incompatible with a conceptually reductive materialism, and *this* upshot, is perhaps not surprising. (If we point out to the reductive materialist that he violates the ordinary conceptual scheme, he may well reply that he is only too ready to do so. In taking this stance he is, to be sure, not inconsistent, but he does cut himself off from participation in those discusions that take place within the mentalistic framework of our standard conceptual scheme.)

On this theory, the conceptual instruments mind uses in its representations of reality are seen not only as *mind-made* (this point – though true – is altogether trivial), but as in various respects *mind-patterned*, and so reflective of their mentalistic origin (noomorphism). The conceptual devices mind deploys for constructing its view of reality are themselves heavily imbued – in the final analysis – with reference to the workings of mind. And it is this fact of the *analytical* fundamentality of mind-invoking (mentalese) conceptions – and not any considerations regarding its causal origins – that render mind basic to matter *in the conceptual order.*

# Conclusion

## A SUMMARY OVERVIEW

It seems appropriate by way of conclusion to review in brief and summary form the principal import and upshot of the preceding discussion.

We have expounded the thesis of *conceptual* idealism, stressing the mind-invoking character of the basic concepts used throughout the standard view of the world as a plurality of concrete particulars located in space and time and interacting causally. Most of the key elements operative in the indicated conceptual scheme (particularity, causal lawfulness, space and time, etc.) have been argued to be such that their full analysis somewhere along the line involves a reference to minds and their capabilities. (Moreover stress has been put upon the strange and far-fetched character that must inevitably attach to any conception of an *an sich* reality described in terms altogether free of any mind-involving conceptions.)

Such a conceptual idealism certainly does not impede the prospects of a physicalist/materialist world-view on the side of causal explanation. It does, however, insist that this causal picture itself cannot be articulated without deploying mind-invoking conceptions (primarily the concepts of lawfulness and causality).

Accordingly, mind appears in a role fundamental even for our concept of 'extra-mental reality,' though just in the hermeneutic order of conceptual clarification, and not necessarily in the order of ontology or of causal explanation.

But, given that it is *not* an ontological theory about the nature of ultimate reality – and, in particular, a theory drastically at odds with materialism – just what does conceptual idealism actually amount to? What it amounts to is, at bottom, not a doctrine as to the nature of reality itself, but one as to the nature of our *thought* about reality – and specifically about the framework of concepts by whose means our view of the world is (standardly) articulated. By insisting upon the paradigmatic role of the

o

experienced phenomenology of mind at this, the *conceptual* level, the conceptualistic version of idealism maintains the traditional idealistic doctrine of the primacy of the mental for our view of the world. But it manages to do so without in any way dictating – as the traditional idealists (in both spiritualist and phenomenalist camps) were wont to do – what the actual content of this view regarding the substantive character of 'ultimate reality' must be on the side of causal explanation.

Mind is on this approach held to be basic not just *for* the conceptualizing of reality (that is quite trivially true), but also *in* our conceptualizing of it. One arrives at the *categorial* fundamentality of mind, in that minds and their capabilities provide reference-points for the framework of concepts we standardly use in the accounts by which we render the make-up and the workings of the world intelligible to ourselves.

It has been argued here that the key ingredients of the standard view of the world as a melange of physical particulars located in space and time and interacting causally are all articulated through mind-invoking conceptions. But just where does this analysis leave us? Its main upshot is clearly this, that insofar as it is conceived of in mind-invoking terms, a thing cannot 'actually and really' – if these be taken in an objective and altogether mind-independent sense – be as it is conceived. And it follows at once that if our analysis is correct, and particularity, space, time, and causality are indeed mind-invoking concepts, then the traditional central thesis of idealism must be accepted: objective reality – if construed in altogether mind-independent terms – is not and cannot be – 'just as' we think of it (and the only reality worth discussing is not reality *per se*, but reality as-we-think-of-it). For insofar as these basic building blocks of our standard view of nature are mind-invoking, a correspondence theory of reality encounters the roadblock that mind-independent reality in principle cannot correspond identically to any mind-invoking view of it. And this means that the boundary separating appearance and reality must be revised. The relationship between the real and the apparent cannot be understood on the ontological lines of a correspondence theory, and must be redrawn along coherentist lines, as a distinction not between 'our' (phenomenal/theoretical) reality and a reality *an sich* (lying wholly outside the phenomenal/theoretical sphere), but as a distinction to be drawn wholly *within* 'our' theoretico-phenomenal realm.

As a matter of principle, the justification of such a framework of mind-invoking concepts cannot be provided by showing that 'it actually corresponds to strictly transcendent (mind-independent) reality.' Such a 'correspondence' to an altogether mind-independent reality is infeasible in the very nature of the thing once our terms of reference are seen as mind-invoking. The validation of an extra-mental deployment of mind-invoking conceptions can only come in pragmatic terms. In the final analysis, our conceptual idealism is thus led to take a pragmatic turn, and to see the ultimate justification of a mind-invoking framework of concepts not in the unworkable terms of an isomorphism with an 'altogether mind-independent reality *an sich*,' but in terms of its capacity to serve successfully the practical aims that underlie man's endeavors to develop and systematize a theoretical rationale for understanding the ways of the world.

# NAME INDEX

# SUBJECT INDEX